PRIVATE SCHOOLS IN INDIA AND THEIR TEACHERS

THE AUTHOR

Binay Laha was born at Srikrishnapur in Durgapur Sub-Division, West Bengal. He has authored many books. His book *"Act local think global"* has been an asset for those who believe to become a global citizen. He is the editor of *Indology,* the English magazine that promotes literature and history. His present book *"Private Schools in India and Their Teachers"* is the outcome of his bitter and fair experience of his teaching which he considers to be a vocation. He has been in teaching for more than a decade. As a private school teacher he has faced many obstacles in teaching right from financial aspect to life threat by management people at a school in Uttar Dinajpur District, West Bengal.

He has graduated from TDB College, Raniganj, West Bengal. Then post-graduated from University of Burdwan and IGNOU with first class. He has pursued MPhil. from Raiganj University. He is a PhD Scholar now.

Apart from his teaching career he has a long literary career of no less than twenty years. He has written in nearly all major dailies in West Bengal right from *Ananda Bazaar Patrika* to *Uttar Banga Sangbad,* and in *The Statesman* nearly 300 times in the open forum on various socio-cultural and educational and political issues among them maximum were on private schooling system. His poems and articles have been published in nearly 200 magazines. His research articles have been published in various national journals and he has taken part in many national, local and international seminars. He has a wide range of interest in reading and travelling. He has already travelled nearly fifteen states of India and three countries. He had been invited at Bhutan's Writers meet. He is associated to Pashim Banga English Academy as a founder Secretary. He is associated to POL magazine of England. He has nearly 15 books in his credit. Adding to this he has been invited and taken part in Television programs in Kolkata and taken part in various debates in Lead Delhi and in various social media groups.

PRIVATE SCHOOLS IN INDIA AND THEIR TEACHERS

BINAY LAHA

ABHIJEET PUBLICATIONS
NEW DELHI 110002

ABHIJEET PUBLICATIONS
4658-A, First Floor, Ambika Bhawan,
21 Ansari Road, New Delhi 110002
Phone: 011-23259444
E-mail: abhijeetpublication@gmail.com
twitter:- @AbhijeetPub21
whatsapp:- 8076785356
instagram: @abhijeet_publications
LinkedIn: jitendra-singh-7729292b/

PRIVATE SCHOOLS IN INDIA AND THEIR TEACHERS

First Published 2022

ISBN 978-93-92816-04-8

PRINTED IN INDIA

Published by J.K. Singh for Abhijeet Publications, New Delhi-110002, Lasertypeset by Abhijeet Typesetters, New Delhi and Printed at Milan Enterprises, New Delhi.

Dedicated to all the Private School Teachers in India

Private School Teacher

Binay Laha

Your work is over.
Now you may go.
What a funny thing.
Ho Ho Ho.

You may be old.
You may be young.
Stand still.
To listen the ding dong dong.

No emotion I find.
Promotion and demotion are the same.
You are just a beggar.
I repeat it once again.

Ministry has never thought.
Never will they think.
Their part they have taken.
The rest is empty ring.
Even god is silent.

He knows everything.
No time will define.
No singer will sing.

Back to its goal.
The clever moves positive.
If you disobey.
You will become fugitive.

You remain peak to your performance.
You are a damn zero.
But if you have right setting.
You are a hero. You are a hero.

Foreword

I have received the manuscript of Binay Laha's book "Private Schools in India and Their Teachers" few months back. I am glad to receive it from him. It gives me immense pleasure to write down few lines on his book as I have seen him since years of how he is with the struggling entities of India. It is indeed a fact that private school teachers in India are suffering a lot from many years ago. Recently Covid 19 has shown the ugly sides of the private school management though few of them have shown humanitarian ground. India, the largest democracy of the world, is in crisis in so far as the private school education is concerned.

Binay Laha has rightly put the differentiation of the private schools in two categories out of them ninty five percent schools are in one category and on the other hand the five percent of the private schools belong to exceptional categories. The exploitation of the teachers have become an unfinished novel of suffering since their joining as a school teacher in his or her locality or to serve far away from their home in search of butter and bread and respect.

It is matter of high honour while I read Binay Laha has chosen this profession as a vocation. In country like India it is difficult to make this profession as a vocation which was a subject of ancient teachers in India.

Every chapters of this books have been written with realistic description of the teachers, management, students and the patrons in historical and sociological base. Binay Laha has thoroughly observed and read the psychology of the said for a long period of time in his life. This picture is nearly same in every part of India. He is fearless to come to the streets for the rights of the private school teachers in India. I have seen him personally to remain active for a national organization day and night despite of his personal loss. He is a successful National Spokesperson. While I acted as the National President I was just robust to bring discipline among our fraternity, in which I have crossed many decades and saw the falling stars, but at the same time I was clearly watching the positive vibes among few of our friends who can fetch help for others.

In his book "Private schools in India and their teachers" Binay Laha has tried to show a ray of hope for the millions of private school teachers in India. I have seen very less work on this particular topic, indeed this book is rare and magnanimous.

I have the opportunity to read some of his other works also. His book *"The Wife of red soil"* and, *"Act local think global'* is mesmerizing. His English magazine *Indology* is having a bright domain in the field of Indian English literature.

He has clear vision to crystalise the education system of India. He is neutral to discuss the points of the management and the realities of their teachers. It is indeed the management who think the teachers as theirs, not as ours to show the proximity of relationship which invites alienation for biasness of treatment.

Most importantly he felt for the masses. He cried for the masses and he is adamant to smile for the entire private school teachers of our India.

As a senior most teacher I would like to say that in many of my years I have felt the same thing in my life.

Binay Laha's book *"Private School Teachers in India and Their Teachers"* is scintillating, non compromising and futuristic.

Regards

Pankaj Bhalla

Karnal, Haryana.

17/09/2021

Acknowledgements

I have gone through many problems and possibilities in my life. But I have never lost hope in humanity, at large. I have spent a decade in the field of private school teaching and learnt every moment from students, teachers, managent and from patrons of the schools. These all moments and experiences have helped me in crystallising my research on Private schools in India and their teachers. I am indebted to all my teachers who taught me to become a teacher. It is their knowledge and aspirations which helped me to become an avid reader who understands the meaning of struggle in his life. I am indebted to all my Teachers at Srikrishnapur Junior High School which was a private school. There I learnt my English alphabet when I reached in class five. I am thankful to Ujjal Nayak Sir, Gosain babu, Bodhan sir, Rabilal Sir, Debdulal Sir, Sanjay Sir and Subhas Sarkar Sir without their teaching I could never been able to read English and write in English as a writer. Similarly I am thankful, in my professional career, to many private school teachers and some of the government school teachers. I am thankful to a madam, whose name I have forgotten, who first gave me the idea to quit from that school which was the first school I have taught because it was she who has opened up my door to catch a better job. So I smiling left that school in Durgapur, West Bengal. I wish thank Late Gulab Sharma of BMSS, Kishanganj, Bihar, who told me to learn everything slowly and silently. I remember him who always used to say me, *Agar aap government sectors me janay chahate hai to ek plan banaye or agar aap private sector met rehnachahate hay to dusra plan banaye* -means if you wish move to government sector, you should make a plan, and if you wish to survive in private sector, then take a different strategy. He was such a lovely man who has never obstructed my increment like others have tried to do. I can remember that he had mentioned many times at the BMSS canteen, while we used to take lunch, regarding our train journey to Balia in Uttar Pradesh and then to Jammu in which I have offered him samosa going to his compartment in the general sleeper class and I was in a air-conditioned class. Many times he has shared me this story that I was in AC compartment. Actually it was odd for me to listen it from my Principal Sir who was a very down to earth and simple man who used to take out the comb from his pocket and comb his hair through the glass of his bike before joining his office everyday. I am thankful to those school management with whom or under whom I have worked undisturbed. I am thankful to Bimal Mittal, who from a management part, asked me about Charles Dickens. I remembered I answered very smartly adding to it that Charles Dickens was the first writer of England to write for the downtrodden class. He became very happy of my reply, so I was selected. I felt BMSS to be my second home. I am indebted to Asha Arora madam, the old teacher who helped to understand to not to run away from troubles. Similarly I should mention Sharbani

Banerjee madam from whom I have learnt to remain quiet and tackle the situation tactfully. So nicely she used to handle her post in my tenure of teaching there. I am really grateful to nearly all hostel teachers with whom I have a prolonged disturbing nights of hope and despair. I can not forget Partho Singha Roy, Ashis Das, Sanjeev Kumar, Samidh Biswas, Bhaskar J. Paul, Koushik Sharma, Nirmalya Roy, Abhishek Jha, Indranil Roy, Dipak Paul, Rony Mondal, Anitangshu Karmakar, Pokhraj Saha, Sarabjit Kaur, Ajanta Sanyal, Manoj Bhagat, Dibyendu Pal, Chanchal Giri, and many others whose name I have forgotten. I will remain ungrateful if I don't admit the contribution of Dr B. Tripathi whose calm behaviour was the response of many silent troubles. Typically I have had to move to different parts of my country. I am indebted to Monika Sharma, of GGCOE, Jammu and Kashmir, who helped me to become more intimated to the college I have studied. I am really grateful to Saroj Sarkar whose spirit, courage and idealism I like most like I am having similar course of discussion with Nausad Ali regarding the improvement of the education at BMS, Raiganj. Similarly I should mention Rina Biswas, of Asansol, whose bold logic I admire. Later on when I get connected to the private school teachers movement India I became acquainted to Rajyabardhan Singh, who is from Gorakhpur, Uttar Pradesh, had been a tremendous source of support for joining hands for the better growth of teachers in India. Adding to this I have got many helps in shaping up my ideas to write this book. Pankaj Bhalla had shown me the way to be a collector of data. He is from Haryana. I learnt the courage to fight once again from the iron lady Principal Tejinder Kaur who is from Punjab. I have learned from a man of Karnataka Vijay Mahanteswar Hosur who has magical organisational power always kept me motivated. His substance of words along with Jagadiwsar Biradar's Gandhian notion of progress were really fantastic. I learned the true meaning of sacrifice from him. Smriti Sharma of Meerat is having so cordial venture that used to really boost up to bring normalcy to the situation when a hot debate was raised in the NEC. I can not deny the importance of Indranil Banerjee who may be older than me but he balances the opinions cooler when I became older to pass it. Shirsendu Chakraborty has helped me in many ways in giving me suggestions and support. His vast experience to move from Assam to Noida helped me in understanding the truth of Indianness. I am grateful to Rajiv Ranjan Sharma, the senior most teacher at DPS whose guidance I will never forget. I shall add Homnath Poudyal of Manipur whose incessant effort to connect the teacher from north east became a gateway for me to understand the suffering and present status of the teachers. My loveliest friend from Orissa Sunil Lima has been a constant source for many reasons. Mithun Das and I felt nearly same problems for many years as we have worked together in the same atmosphere. Mithun Chandra Ghosh and I were energetic to come to the streets for teachers rights. I am indebted to him for my venture. As my book deals with the problems and possibilities of the private schools in India I was robust in interacting with many teachers. I might have missed out many names but surely would remain grateful to everyone who have shown me the way.

At the same time I am indebted to all the contributors who contributed their reactions upon my works. Those beloved students, teachers, school owners and Parents have Co operated me in completing my venture. Nurul from Bangladesh has sent me his articles on nearly the same situation in his country. I just wanted to fetch a comparison. That virtual meeting with Nurul enriched me a lot.

I wish to thank Priyaranjan Paul, of Raiganj Coronation High School, one of the most reputed school of West Bengal, for his incessant inspiration and support for every cause of the private school teachers. Though he is a government school teacher he had never ignored our subtle problems. He always wanted a change of this situation whenever I have talked to him regarding it. Many others government teachers have helped me in shaping my concept. Dr Ratan Ghosh is one of them. Dr Gaurango Mahanta, an avid reader and a wonderful writer of Bangladesh and a Civil Servant, who advised me to study few things and to work with all dedication. I do always get help from Uday Shankar Durjay, who is a resident of England, regarding literature to private schooling system in England and many more things without any much hesitation. I thank him.

While I write any book I become a sangsarbairagi, I mean indifferent to family life, in this case, I remained undisturbed in all transitional experience because of my wife and of my daughter. I am ever grateful to them. Sad to add that when I was about to complete my work I was suffering for a fatty lump grown upon my right hand adjacent to my shoulder. It was bleeding time and again till it was operated by Dr Kalishankar Bhattacharya, whose daughter has been taught by me a decade ago at a CBSE school. I thank my doctor also.

I am thankful to Dr Ray for whom I have been able to understand the uses of sentences, in exact temperament, and in picking up a topic in which I can at least contribute better than others.

I am thankful to many professors who have helped me in enhancing my writing skills because I believe that I am a weak writer.

Many discussions have taken place in between me and my friend Joyprakash Sharma who has taught in Bhutan for few years. I have heard from him many good things of the private schooling system in Bhutan. In comparison to Indian Private Education System I have been able to find out the international proximity to teaching and the policy of the management which is nearly same, in some cases good in India, in some cases good in Bhutan, but it is the belief of both the souls that India is a wonderful hub of private school education. It is a pleasure that I have got chance to work with him and found a noble soul. Apart from this prolonged discussion with him regarding the education school education system in Bhutan and in India with him, we have tried to surrender to a entrepreneurial venture in Kolkata. Though it became a failure. But our discussions continue for many years as he has been teaching in different parts of India. For understanding the pan Indian scenario his contribution to my ideas is immense.

I am thankful to all the critics of my life because it is for them I find solutions in problems but they find problems in every solution. It is for them I remain mostly creative as they love to stop my voice. We live in the largest democracy of the world. So to accept them is my civility.

Last but not least I am really thankful to Wikipedia and other sources of internet, whatsapp for collecting many primary sources like the affiliation bye laws of CBSE, ICSE including Macaulay Minutes. I got pleasure when many of my letters and articles regarding private schools and the suffering of the teachers have been published by *Anandabazar Patrika* and in *Uttar Banga Sambad*. It was the ray of hope that my messages are being read by lakhs of people. I can not but thank them.

I thank those victimised teachers who communicated to us through epistolary correspondence because their pains became my pain.

I thank my father late Sannyasi Laha whose many similarities I bear as I find a similar genetic base with him to have a will remain as sportive like him in different spectrum.

I don't claim it to be an original research work but I have tried my level best to use my personal experiences, conversations, reactions, letters to the different government bodies, minutes of different organizations, and few books for serving the purpose. Indeed it is a Himalayan task to write a book on the holistic Private Schools in India and their teachers. My work is very little one. I don't have much perseverance even to write for years. This may be called as a history book with socio economic pattern of the lives of the private school teachers in India. May not be also. I will remain apologetic, in advance, if I have forgotten to admit anybody's contribution to complete my work. This work will be a significant one if the readers do find a similar situation in India in understanding "Private schools in India and Their Teachers".There may remain mistakes and errors in the book, despite hard attempts to weed them out, readers and well wishers are requested to point out them to me, and in next edition they will be rectified.

I wish to thank Abhijeet publications and JK Singh sir for their incessant support to publish this book. Without their effort my work would not become materialsed.

Binay Laha

Raiganj, West Bengal, India.

Preface

After attending an international literary meet at Varanasi I went to Allahabad few years back. I travelled different parts of Allahabad. But till ever I did not have any friends from teaching background. Later on I got the opportunity to meet virtually and physically to many friends throughout Uttar Pradesh, one of the largest populated state of India. Many lakhs of private school teachers are surviving in this profession. This is such a state from where I met one of the Principal under whose guidance I have learnt so many things in my life. Actually my entry to the rest of India became possible for this man for whom I have lamented in one of the article.

But before mixing with the pan Indian friends my life was confined to west Bengal only .After completing my post graduation I came to North Bengal, the northern part of West Bengal.

North Bengal, the integral part of West Bengal, has crossed many hurdles in between 1947 to the present span of time. This part of North Bengal was actually a part of Rahshahi Division of India. Only Darjeeling district was a part of North Bengal since the first day of Independence. The fate of Jalpaiguri, Malda and Dinajpur were decided not on 15 august 1947 as the Radcliffe Line was published on 17 august. So finally on 17 august these three districts became a permanent part of west Bengal in India after the Independence of India. Kuch Bihar, as a district, became a part of west Bengal on 1 st January 1950. Dinajpur became Paschim Dinajpur after it became a part of West Bengal, the other major part of Dinajpur included in Bangladesh. So there were five districts Darjeeling, Jalpaiguri, Cooch Behar, Malda and Paschim Dinajpur in North Bengal in between 1947 to 1991 while Pashim Dinajpur was bifurcated into Uttar and Dakshin Dinajpur. Later Kalimpong was separated from Darjeeling and Alipurduar became a new district after her political divorce to Jalpaiguri. Similary South Bengal have got many new district. Durgapur, Which was once a part of undivided Bardhaman District, included in Pashim Bardhaman with all her exuberance and spontaneity. Durgapur was that city from where I completed my class twelve and graduation at TDB college, Raniganj which is hardly 22 kilometers away from Durgapur through bus route.

I took my primary education at my ancestral village Srikrishnapur in the Durgapur Sub division. My upper primary school was a private one and it was a tribal school by her name. Srikrishnapur Junior Tribal School was her name. The name has been kept such to get affiliation swiftly. However it has never got affiliated. I have felt the insecurity of those teachers who use to teach us. Finally the school was closed down due to many factors. It shifted to adjacent Majhipara which is a part of our village. However I got my best education in my life in the upper primary stage. After crossing upper primary at my village I passed class ten from Gourbazar Rampada High school.

The idea to write this book "*Private Schools and Their Teachers* came during lockdown while we all faced very difficult situation like joblessness or half payment or no payment at all. We have seen many private school teachers to change their professions like school principal to a idli seller or to become a daily labour .Lock down has shook the fate of lakhs of private school teachers in India. I have spent many sleepless nights thinking for our beloved fraternity, who are actually suffering not only from lock down period but also since India has got political freedom from the British. But I wish to add that my school has never given half payment, during lock down, we all have got regular full payment, though not as per norms. But it is indeed philanthropic to motivate us by giving payment while more fifty percent in India, in a rough calculation, have not given even payment to their teachers. Many thousand teachers have been gifted Termination due shortage of fund. No government has stood with the private school teachers. I just tried to reduce my pain by writing the suffering of the teachers.But before lock down we have been very active in forming CITO for the private school teachers in West Bengal and later on to the rest of India. Seven teachers, primarily decided to come to the street for shouting louder on 5th August 2019. We have been supported by many teachers. CITO is indeed the first private school teachers organisation to come to the street in west Bengal and India also. Many organizations are limited to only whatsapp revolutions. We were fearless to face the reality. PVT of Gorakhpur led by Rajyabardhan Singh saw us an added ray linked to it by S Prasad who happens to be my colleague but later on shifted to Uttar Pradesh. A silking enthusiasm I got from a team from entire India in nearly twenty four states. Vijay Mahantesh A Hosur was a noble heart from Karnataka I discovered and connected to him, indeed it was godly to get our team. So nicely we became known to each other. We were confirmed that whatever had to be done had to be done by us only. We have avoided politicians. But nothing can be separated from politics. In Karnataka Former Prime Minister H.D. Devegowda joined the private school teachers organisation to support. But gone into vain. Politicians were vocal to lucrative proposal for their vote bank but they remained silent for the private school teachers as they the teachers failed to create a big organisation to create a vote bank.

I have got the opportunity to read many books during this period as I did not have any other work rather than the online classes for my school. I have read throughly *Argumentative Indian* by Nobel Laureate Amartya sen and his memoir *"Home in the world"*. Books of Eric Hobsbawm, Romila Thapar, Markanday Katju, Leila Seith, Kautilya, Satish Chandra, Rup Kumar Barman, Suranjan Das, Swaraj Basu, *Bhagavatgita*, Upanishads, *Quran*, Ranjan Chakraborty, Nilakantha Sastri, Kaushik Basu, Shashi Tharoor, J. L. Nehru, R. Rolland, N. Roy, Aristotle, William Darlymple, Jean Dreze,, S. Mukherjee, Emily Dickinson, Pranab Bardhan, Tapan Roychowdhury, Ayesha Jalal, Thomas A. Timberg, Romain Rolland, Ruskin Bond, Khuswant Singh, G. Palanithurai, Shahid Amin, Whelpton, IBn Battuta, A. Kapoor, Manish Sisodia, Nayantara Sahgal, Maulana Azad, Chittabrata Palit, Peter Frankopan and many others. These all books help me in crystallising my thoughts to write a book.

Apart from reading books I got interest in listening or taking part in debates. Various media persons I like most. Out of them Pranoy Roy, Rajdeep Sardesai, Arnab Goswami, Barkha dutt, Suman Dey, Moupia Nandy, Ravish Kumar are excellent Indian media persons. I have learnt and motivated by them. I feel relaxed to listen Kumar Biswas. Whenever I hear his Hindi verses I just return back to love my mother tongue Bengali. They all helped to find indianness in my topic. I could have written this book in Bengali in a much sofisticated loftiness for my command over Bengali but I have chosen English, though as a weak writer with many grammatical errors, to just to send my words to all private school teachers in entire India as I believe English is such a language which has united India as well as the globe despite its many hegemony since the colonial period.

On the other hand first few months of lockdown has kept me busy in organisational work too. I have worked as the state president of West Bengal and at the same time I have been given the charge of National Spokesperson by the same organization. I have learnt a lot from this organization. This organization has given me the lesson to become a selfless and then a selfish and vice versa. It was just like Shakespeare's "Fair is foul, and foul is fair".

The title of this book has been modified and then given the sub title "their teachers" to show the alienation from the school and then from the teachers. Indeed the owners do not treat their teachers as their own until required.

The book has been written for our educated generation .Every citizens of India do have the right to know why are the private school teachers are suffering since colonial intervention to the capitalist venture. I will remain highly greatful if this my little effort helps in the growth of Indian education system. I have decided to donate some percent of profits of this book for the motivation of the private school teachers at Indology Literary Meet which I am organizing since 2018.

Binay Laha

Raiganj, West Bengal

Contents

1

Introduction

Where the mind is without fear.

And the head is held high.

——Rabindranath Tagore

This is my common observation that nearly all private school teachers in India have at least once been terminated from school or they have left their jobs out of disappointment. Personally I don't like education to be imparted in private mode in India. But so far as our country has failed to control population explosion after independence we find always a situation of crisis of proper service in each sector, either in health or in education, specially in the public sector. There are huge pressure in government schools in India. Students receive their education without maintaining any ratio like 40:1 or 35:1. On the other hand private schooling system in India started in the ancient times. India has received private schooling since the Gurukulam system or the system of pathshala to use it to its best level either through individual effort or by the patronisation of the kings. This is no wonder that ancient students received much natural studies of life,

Atman or self observation through the study of Vedas or Upanishads, Puranas etc. One can not ignore to mention the spiritual education of the *alvars* saints in southern part of India though it was not formal one. But they have been able to unite the masses to bring peace and harmony. India is a land of spiritual gurus. Here people learnt bhakti through different great saints of India. Guru Nanak, Kabir Das have motivated Indians for non materialistic gaining and secular study. India has a long tradition and legacy of education which may be older than the European system of Education. The students at Bologna University, one of the oldest running university of the world has started their classrooms in the open nature. Students used to sit under the tree. In world famous Oxford University too has cultivated similar experience during the medieval period in England. Education was precious every where. During Colonial period too seen better growth of private English medium schools in different parts of India by the help of the Christian missionaries. They wanted to give western knowledge and light to the Indian students. The passing of Macaulay Minute 1835 was a landmark milestone for the promotion of civilising Indians, which I found baseless and tricky to make Indians down, in may ways help Indians to get clerical jobs for the benefit of the British, but in consequence it became boomerang as Indians do have an indomitable spirit and zeal to learn and capture our position holding job of civil servants and etcs but at the same time it opened up many school teaching jobs. Macaulay was of the opinion of the closure of the pathshala system of education in India. But both were running simultaneously as it runs today both in vernacular and in English medium schools. But predominantly English medium schools have been dominating in the field of Indian schooling system. That is the choice of the citizens and the need of the hour.

It is not possible for government to create jobs for everybody. But it is not impossible to promote education through government mode only. There is the conspiracy of the capital economy which has made the walk of the government much palpable. Liberalisation was such venture that gave power to the capitalist to loot the private education system which has been described rightly by Kunwar Rajyabardhansingh as the *lootera* class. But I don't find always a distinction in between philanthropy and lootera. This is a matter of great wonder that the unworthy exploitation in the education field is given birth to Capital Economy which was not the promise of the government to set such boards to promote education for the benefits of society at large. How can the boards ignore their duties to protect the teachers? How can a school pay a teacher only eight thousand rupees per month as his /her salaries in an affiliated English medium schools despite of the presence of the board? Why the teachers are signing in such a register which does not match with the register submitted to the account office or shown to government? How can we say that the government officials and other machineries are not corrupted? Why then are we teaching to the students the idealism of Mahatma Gandhi or Subhas Chandra Bose? What will the students learn when he or she saw his beloved teachers were terminated or left the school before their examination out of despair ?Is not it the sum total loss of entire education process? The answer is with you. I just want to say that putting on a bright tie and coat in the school campus for showing eliticism has no connection to education but this is an added slavery to western hegemony and culture. We don't have to copy the western culture to make ourselves a mimic. But government should not fetch mimicry to the teachers being so indifferent in their problems. Who will listen to the problems of the private school teachers in India? In every 24 hours a teacher is terminated in this sector which is my observation. It is a kind of mental assault. But who will care for them? The lock down has shown much robust situation for them.

Many parents were signing petition for "No School No fees". But the Online classes were on and still continuing. This was the major strike and provocation to observe the attitude of the society towards private school teachers. Financial Crises were there during lockdown in every part of India and broadly to the rest of the world. But Education in private institutions are not stopped. It is continuous from the day one of the lockdown. Have ever they thought of teachers' payment? I have gone through the bye laws of CBSE and ICSE which have clearly mentioned that a private school has to keep a sufficient fund. However the Managent has already turned problems into possibilities. They are the business class apart from few schools management belong to philanthropist. But the number of philanthropists in this sector is very less. So generally the teachers are suffering as they are paid half or not paid at all for many months. Teachers are having lot of financial burden like the other entity of the society. Government is taking no responsibility for the teachers in the private institutions even in regard to implement the rules. Government always take care of Govt employees. They are paid for months without any regular work which we have seen during lock down.Thanks to the government for taking care of her employees so nicely and elegantly. This is a naked truth that the teachers in the private institutions, specially in schools, are deprived since the dawn of education in India. In ancient time also teachers have been given enough respect but not enough money. Teachers belonged to the poor classes of people. During Colonial intervention we have seen a better picture of the private English medium school teachers in India but this was reserved to the Europeans, at large. Teachers in the English medium schools were recruited through christian missionaries. As in consequence, many good schools set up to promote western light and knowledge. The biggest downfall came up after the nineties while the liberalisation started up in India. The private schools in India has been shifted from the colonial intervention to the Capitalist venture. The rich people began investing money to establish private schools without thinking about their teachers in true sense of term. The lock down has seen the end of humanitarian zeal of the few management. Thousands of teachers remained starved as their income became half or nil for months. Shifting their vocations became a common choice as survival is mostly important than prestige. It is pathetic to read that a private school principal started selling fruits for sustainability. Nearly every one read that a teacher from Bihar became a labour to earn money as his account remained empty for his school has not paid him for months. As a part of this fraternity, I can remember, I announced, as a spokesperson of an organization, that we are ready to help this teacher. But we could not been able to find his address. Many incidences have happened, in consequence, we could not resist to tear for our fellow teachers. The situation is improving little bit but the basic pattern is nearly the same. Teachers are coping up with new reality like painful virtual classes are on. In my personal life I have grown up by the help of both government school teachers and private school teachers. I have seen the suffering of the my private school teachers closely. I have been many private school teachers to loose their jobs in the end of twentieth century. And in transition I have started my career as a private school teacher in my hometown

Durgapur in the beginning of the twenty first century. I am indeed a product of twentieth century and twenty first century. Since my studentship I have been conscious about the lives of the private school teachers. I always salute them for they are the reasons lakhs of students in India are getting professional success and earning as per their expectations. But nearly ninty five percent, roughly, as my calculations comes through many debates and observations, do not get the chance to lead a better lives. But why? If, there is a rule, it must be implemented by the state and the central government. Otherwise policy of adjustment or a separate Private school service commission must be implemented so that no school will be able to pay below that amount if they are able to pay as per norms. Treating a private school teacher as a facilitator is derogatory and it must be stopped. Use and throw policy, is used in nearly all private schools, except few, specially the senior most old teachers who have sacrificed their entire lives getting nothing at all, brings the shadow picture of our education system. We often say, Guru Brahma, Guru Bisnu means we consider them as deity but in reality, we treat them narrowly as they can not earn than their expectation. I have heard many nasty things fetched upon them.Even by many government school teachers who send their children to the hand of a private school teacher but ignore their contribution and blamed them as "quality less" human being. How long will we have to tolerate this attitude of the society? One more thing I wish to add that whenever I have gone to quest my query regarding private school teacher to a district education officer they just wash the dust from their shirts and said this is not their matter and this is matter of the central government. And when a teacher writes to the central government they say it belongs to the state. Wonderful indeed. Happy to read when a retired government teacher is disturbed to get pension, the court orders the state to suspend the education office who is connected to it. But when a private school teacher is terminated after ten years of his teaching it became only a story of a tea adda. It does not reach to the *Sushil Samaj* or to the *Budhhijibi* of our Nation. They only love to criticize the government for lucrative popularity they may get in the media and among the people. Government should take these problems of the nation building private school teachers, all excellent students are reading in the private schools, except few,with care for the greater future of India. How long will the government remain indifferent knowing everything. But I am very hopeful. I am sure that the cloudy days will be over and the private school teachers in India will get a better shining of sun in favour of them. I believe that argumentation is important to get a viable atmosphere for better education and better lives of the teachers. Teachers should not be afraid to face the challenge of being alone because ages after it is Indian teachers and reformers fought for the rights. Our country is having a wonderful base of logic and argument. This country has produced many female intellectual who loved to argue to establish their point when the rest of world were anxious to give voice to the female. Our education system is itself is within the process of radicalism as we live in the best form of democracy, if not like America, which I believe a better platform for global democracy. Contemporary Intellectual like Amartya Sen, the Nobel Laureate, who as a teacher, remained mostly non compromising whenever there is a problem of the policy making which is not for the welfare of the people of India. I can give many examples of teachers who left government jobs and joined in the private institutions. Teachers need to come out from any kind of frustration and they should take legal help if required for their survival. Collective effort may serve better in this perspective. Teachers should talk directly to the management or if they don't listen then to District education officer and even if he does not put ear to it one should move to the constitution. I have got personal benefit out of this process. Teachers may take the help of social media which may help in many regards. At least teachers should not return back to home without any sufficient cause. Better teaching atmosphere is our right.Better nation is our dream. So we should not let others to disrupt our service because it may demotivate the students also. It is the teachers who always help students in overcoming their problems, then why not they should solve their problems in right order. Leaving the school, in frustration and disappointment, is an advantage for the management. A great thing may happen if the private schools teachers jointly take loans from bank and open up a school for entrepreneurial venture and make their journey smother than before. This may create job opportunities and best education opportunity as whatever the blame we put upon the management may turn to be a testimony. Many private teachers in their life have struggled to open up school and remained successful in doing so. I know a teacher who was terminated from a big school became successful in setting up a big school like his former destination in kishanganj. Indeed the school in which I teach presently is owned by a teacher who established this school forty three years ago. This is oldest English medium school of this district having all streams in senior secondary section. This is not impossible. We At the same time if we can not take such temperament we should apply those things in our lives that we teach proudly in the classroom. We are habituated to see Bagha

Jatin as our neighbour, but not as our own family members. Before ending up the introductory part one can not ignore to say the need to promote the spiritual link in between teachers, managent, students and the patrons as always we prove to remain social. So the peace order is important. The spiritual conscious is the ultimate value of life though we understand it in different stages. If we cultivate the spiritual lesson of Gautam Budhha and specially his Eightfold path,,many problems may automatically be solved. The greatest lesson of my life that I have taken from Gautam Budhha is "Our desire is the root cause of all evils" which I, as history post graduate teacher, always love to input into the ear of my beloved students, unnecessarily and necessarily, because I believe that students need to be taught the value education through slow process because we hear that society has nearly rotten up in excessive material pursuit. A son is for getting to take care of his parents and sending them to the Old age home.We have forgotten to create a generation of what Swami Vivekananda dreamt of. A man making world is the best education a student should be imparted through out their schooling because school is much vital than colleges or Universites in shaping up the immature minds and making their personalities. Whatever the base a student will get in a school he will grow up with nearly same vision.

Many great personalities of India had started their school at private school. Raja Rammohan Roy, the modern thinker of India, took his primary education at a pathshala in Bengal. Later on he was studied at a maqtab in Patna. Though this fact remains in confusion for many scholars. At the same time Rabindranath Tagore took his early education at Oriental Seminary which is considered to be the oldest private school in India. B.R. Ambedkar took his early education at Elphinstone, Mumbai. Even Amartya Sen, the greatest intellectual of our time, was admitted to a Christian missionary school in Dhaka which was then a part of Undivided India. World's greatest Cricket Captain Sourav Ganguly took his early education in a private English medium school in kolkata.Indeed thousands of successful Indians were studied in private schools. Arabinda Ghosh, the greatest freedom fighter turned Yogi had studied in a private English medium school in Darjeeling. He is outstandingly famous for his book *The life Divine* and "Savitri". Famous Film actor and singer Anjan Dutta was at St Pauls, Darjeeling. Leila Seth, the first female Indian judge of a high court, educated at Loreto Convent, Darjeeling. Her son Vikram Seth, the eminent Indian English Novelist studied at Doon Public School. Even Visva Bharati which was established by Rabindranath Tagore was a private school. Later on it became a central government university.

Despite of thousand troubles we teachers should not leave up in booming the young minds because we don't know how many great assets may be grown in the hand of the private school teachers.

Last but not the least I wish to add my favourite Shelley," If winter comes, can spring be far behind?"

2

CITO to NGTO

A history of suffering of the private English school teachers in India in the post independence era.

The setting of the silhouette behind all crying of the private English medium school teachers in India is having ambiguity of explanation and assumptions of hope since the independence of India. The British era was much better as it was only meant to them and meant for them. They lived in a separated snobbish world to promote western education and knowledge after the charter act of 1813. This Charter 1813 had liberated Christian missionaries to set up churches and English medium schools in India. It was just like a *dastak* for them. This *dastak* of the Christian missionaries of England has been able to serve two purposes. One is the promotion of Christian religion and the second is the promotion of western knowledge and light in the name of the English education by setting up English medium schools in different parts of India. Many wonderful convent schools have really been successful in promoting English education through the dedication, care and knowledge of the missionaries. It is their sacrifice India has become the second largest English speaking country of the world. But I won't be able to satisfy you if I pick up the condition of the private English medium school teachers in the post independence era as long as their salaries,management pressure, unnecessary and force termination, the indifference of the state as well as central government is concerned. Alas! 95 percent teachers, fairly, hope all teachers will agree to my data, get less than 15 thousand salaries in the affiliated cbse or icse based English medium schools in India. This is a matter of grave shame that they are just treated as anything below to their dignity, if defined them as slave to their management won't sound bad.

English medium schools in India are predominantly affiliated to cbse, icse or by state government. The maximum number of English medium schools fall under cbse which is an autonomous body of the central government. Less You may blame my data to be wrong I should glorify the rest five percent private English medium schools pay higher than the government scale or as per government scale.

The covid 19 period has seen the worst ever situation of the status of the English medium school teachers in India. Only those five percent of the schools have paid their teaching and non teaching staffs seventy to eighty percent of their salary in a rough estimate. The rest ninety five percent of schools have failed to fulfill the minimum salary pattern to their teachers, worst to say, they always have chosen the "road not taken" policy. I mean they are exceptional in manipulating the government system. I do wish to blame to the government equally. It is because of the indifference of the both category of government the private school teachers are suffering and leaving a painful life sans any monetary luxuries which they deserve as per govt norms.

Role of CITO in inviting conciousness among private school teachers :

CITO has played a pivotal role in awakening the private English medium school teachers in West Bengal, though not in a pervasive way as they have been alienated by the same fraternity. The CBSE and ICSE teachers organisation have been formed by me along with few well wishers like Saroj Sarkar, Samidh Biswas, Dipak Paul, Nausad Ali, Bina Biswas, Barun Chakraborty, Dr Late Banibrata Tripthi and others. This entire team of CITO was having more than two hundred teachers through out India. This is the first organization of India to fight for the private English medium school teachers right stepping forward to the street to shout louder openly with banner of CITO in their hand. They kept five demands for the teachers right from the inclusion of pf to each teachers to pay commission and others. The leading newspaper of West Bengal *Ananda Bazaar Patrika* published the movement of CITO. Thanks to ABP. But this movement has become silent soon afterwards. It has tried to their end to raise voice for the injustices happened to Mr Tripathi, a social teacher in Uttar Pradesh. Mr Tripathi has been slapped by a management people inside the school campus. The students in fury fell the school buses on the ground. Here at Raiganj CITO comes to the street for Mr Tripathy. Many thousand people from different corner in India supported this movement online. But after few months more teacher who joined physically to CITO kept themselves aloof from it due to fear or for selfishness like many noble movements have been disrupted in India in this way. However the teacher leaders of CITO was not hopeless.

Emergence of NGTO :

Long after the silence of CITO, the Facebook has given a promotional chance to all the dear one to once again meet with their ill fated destiny. CITO finds the demands of CITO and NGTO are the same. The purpose is the same. The philosophy is the same. But I should mention that one more private teacher organisation came into confession long back within the whatsapp group is PVT Gorakhpur. Personally I call Mr Rajyabardhansingh Kunwar to work jointly for the greater good of the private school teachers in India. He agreed to my proposal but he also became hopeless like CITO faces the same destiny due to non cooperation from the same fraternity. I told Mr Rajyabardhan that we can only bark. However, NGTO became a ray of hope for many months for the teachers in India. The subtle difference that NGTO leads is their holistic inclusion of the entire private teaching and non teaching fraternity right from school to private colleges to private universities in different states of India. The excessive penchant to make this movement an online one virtually gave birth doubt of account, revenues and leadership. But this organization was wonderful in uniting pan Indian teachers. The national meeting of Ngto was really wonderful. Representative from nearly twenty four states used to cover many vital agendas. One of the most active man from Karnataka Mr Vijay Mahantesh A. Hosur singlehandedly raised this organization to great height. He has been a great maestro to unite teachers in the southern part of India. He has been the key factor to enhance the revenues of NGTO to a greater extent. The man of another need from the southern part of India is Jagadiswar Biradar. He is Gandhian by faith. He was ready to sacrifice for NGTO. He has been in severe frustration when he saw that the founder of NGTO is as vague and visionless as he failed to answer the questions of the fellow members of NGTO. Raja Nayakar is another brave soul who wanted a real change in livelihood of the private school teachers.

Comes the dedication of Pankaj Bhalla who has been given the duty of the National President of NGTO. He is really praiseworthy to follow the dictum of NGTO until it goes to falsification of words and became a mere revenue collector. Tajinder Kaur, I should mention her as to be a very honest and noble warrior who never compromised in her carrier as a principal in different reputed schools, played the same role in NGTO till to the faith broken by A. Nagar and V. K. Nagar. I should explain in brief of why Indranil Banerjee, a principal in Indore left NGTO. He has observed NGTO for one long month before he joined here actively. But what he got is the futility of his hard labour and planning for NGTO. He found V. K. Nagar as a fraud and a trickster whose ultimate aim was to anyhow enhance the numbers of the members to get a good account of revenues. Homnath Poudyal from Manipur but settled as a principal in Chhatisgarh has tried his level best to pick up the best teacher leaders from North East. Talliakum, Ananya Chowdhury, Rajib Sharma, Ashish Sarkar have in excellent connection to promote this organization in the North East Area. And obviously from Bengal the same CITO team was always ready to do the needful. The outstanding voice of Saroj Sarkar has become the voices of many teachers in India. Rajib Ghosh Roy was always subtle to put the right logic in which V. Nagar used to be trapped into confusion. Samidh Biswas was another noble soul whose cause to join in NGTO have remained the effect to merge CITO into NGTO.

Binay Laha as a National Spokesperson of NGTO :

I had been a stupid stuff to shout always for NGTO, emotionally and painfully because I was dreaming to make NGTO a stronger organization that will raise every issue of the private school teachers in India. But I was sure that I have able to motivate the representative as a national spokesperson selected by V. K. Nagar. I must thank to Virendra Nagar with whom I have long been associated just like his obedient soldier who later on started triggering for his master. And at the same time I have been cheated by most cunning A. Nagar whose every action used to remain a disqualification as his mal intention vitiated the entire hemisphere. The nice relation with Virendra Tripathi of Varanasi was distorted, if not still to be restored though some messages

A total collapse of CITO and NGTO in helping private teachers in India :

The time and tide spoke reverse as it was our fault to unite properly to all the private school teachers and teachers in the private sector at large. How a beautiful unification of hearts of Indian teachers have been reflected through NGTO. Indeed we should remain greatful to its good time. There is still a need to unite to walk together to reduce the suffering of the private school teachers whom we have seen in lock down to become a labour or idli seller of a fruit seller in the marker. This is indeed a matter of pride while a principal Mrs Smitri Sharma from Meerut does feel the problem and suffering of a private school teacher in west Bengal or Madam Chetna from Delhi raises voices for every body. How can we forget that day when Lead Delhi, the television channels ask us whether we would stop our movement to become a political leaders. We all, Pankaj Bhalla, Tejinder Kaur, Vijay Mahantesh A. Hosur, Binay Laha, were louder to Ajay Jain to stand for Indian private school teachers who are suffering since independence as an orphan. Many number of teachers like Mr Pawan, Mr Kamalesh Sharma, Mr Sanjay Sharma have been patient to get a victory from the teachers part as all have seen the deadliest end of this profession, while oftentimes, it is said that teaching is the last profession to choose, if not true for government sectors, but surly to the private sector.

Last but not the least it should be included that the courage of Shirsensu Mukherjee, the dedication of Dr Dubey will never go in vain. We have seen the partial failure of few organization like CITO, PvT or like NGTO but we have a tremendous positivity that one day the pain and suffering of the teachers in the private institutions will be reduced or reflected on the eye of the government to get the justice.

NGTO MINUTES ARE GIVEN BELOW AS IT WAS COLLECTED FROM THE NEC GROUP WITHOUT ANY CHANGES OF SENTENCES:

Minutes of the meeting held on 26th April 2020

The meeting was hosted by Mr.Birendra Tripathi, President of NGTO(UP) and initiated by Mr.Virendra Nagar, NGTO, National co-ordinator, in which he spoke of

- the mission and vision of NGTO, which is currently encompassing 24 states, 15000 teachers and 1000 active members.
- The organization has been formed keeping in mind the welfare and upliftment of teachers, similar salary, benefits as government teachers.

- To stand for justice and overall development of teachers.
- He also added that the attitude of the society has to change towards teachers.
- The respect towards teachers as was done in the ancient days has to restored.

There was a brief introductory session of the newcomers in this week's meeting, which included Ms. Priyadarshani Sardesai, Principal of a private school in Pune, Mr. Homnath Paudyal, Principal of a private school in Madhya Pradesh, Mr. Rajiv Ranjan, Principal of a private school in Assam, Mr. Pankaj Bhalla, Administrative officer in a private school in Haryana.

The agenda for this week were -

- Membership
- content of the letter to be sent to PMO/CM/NHRD/State Education Minister/Governors/DEO
- Website upgradation

Mr. Alok Nagar suggested that there be a National Planning Committee comprising of 11 members in which based on concensus four were selected which comprised of Ms.Tejinder Pal Singh (Punjab), Mr. Keshav Chhetri (New Delhi), Ms. Priyadarshani Sardesai (Pune) and Ms.Poorva Tiwari (Korba) and rest will be added in due course.

The second agenda was taken up by Mr. Birendra Tripathi, in which he reiterated that-

- Appointment letter should be compulsory, net/gross salary, PF to be mentioned as well as the probation period.

- 12 months salary to be paid.
- No. of periods to be decided as per grade of teacher.
- Medical leaves and all other leaves to be incorporated.
- cc of letter to be given to PMO, CM.
- contribution to be made for NGTO staffs to travel across the country like Shankaracharya, spreading the presence of NGTO.

In this regard Ms. Smriti Sharma added that-

- HRA, DA, TA and other deductions should also be mentioned in the letter.
- There should be a Teacher Welfare Organization in each school.
- she also added that Women Grievance Cell should also be there.

Mr. Vijay Hosur (Karnataka) added that-

- All kind of leaves a teacher is entitled to be mentioned in the letter.
- The salary mentioned should be as per the standard salary prescribed by the government.

Mr. Birendra Tripathi pointed out that, teachers who have joined NGTO must be informed about their rights and that a written data should be circulated in all NGTO groups.

Ms. Smriti Sharma add that

- education of 2 kids to be free of teachers working in a particular school.
- there should not be any one-sided contracts.

- Service Book to be made compulsory for all teachers.
- There should be Leave encashment facility for teachers.

Mr. Birendra Tripathi also stressed that

- this is a fight for rights with the government and not with the management of any school.
- Magazine to be printed by the organization.

In this context Mr.Virendra Nagar/Ms. Smriti Sharma said that for that some registration needs to be done so for the time being we can come out with Newsletters, inwhich teachers can write about Problems in Education and similar issues.

Mr. Pankaj Bhalla said that the Service Rules are not shown to the teachers and is only kept to be shown to the authorities.

Mr. Alok Nagar once again stressed that membership has to increase.

Ms. Smriti Sharma said that to do that there should be a Press Note, teachers to be made aware about NGTO, expenses will be incurred in this regard.

Mr. Chhetri agreed to contribute Rs.5000/- for this cause.

It was decided in the meeting that Ms.Sunita Singh and Mr. Binay Laha will be the media spokesperson for NGTO. Mr. Birendra Tripathi this body to be responsible to give write-ups in newspapers.

Ms. Priyadarshani Sardesai disclosed that many teachers have not been paid 3 months salary in her school as fees have not been recovered.

Ms. Tejinder Pal Singh indicated that ESI details should be mentioned in the appointment letter.

Mr. Rajiv Ranjan sir pointed out the current problems he is facing in Assam where 2nd language has been decided as the local language as a result of which 20,000 Hindi/Sanskrit teachers will be jobless in Assam. He also said that there were some schools which have instructed teachers to join any organization.

Mr.Virendra Nagar stressed that this organization is going to look into all problems faced by teachers.

Mr.Birendra Tripathi stressed that a Press Release to be circulated informing the general public of the formation of NGTO and then a subsequent Press release of the meetings being held.

Mr. Binay Laha informed the members that the information will be circulated to PTI which will ensure circulation in local newspapers. He also stressed on the usage of social media for this purpose, YouTube channel has already been launched by Mr. Alok Nagar in this regard, where teachers can share their own story.

The meeting concluded on a positive note and a promise to fulfill the aspirations of all teachers.

[19:34, 8/30/2021] History: NGTO National Meeting

Minutes of meeting held on 3rd May 2020

The meeting was hosted by Mr. Birendra Tripathi, President of NGTO (UP)

Agenda

1. Review of the last meeting.
2. Action plan of membership in structure manner.
3. NGTO's upcoming news portal.
4. Development of Organization.
5. Introduction of New Members.

The meeting was started with the introduction of new members.

Mr. Homnath Paudyal introduced four active members representing four districts of Manipur.

- In the last meeting the NEC had a thorough discussion on each and every point to be drafted in the letter.
- The letter was forwarded to PMO, New Delhi and to the CM and Chief secretaries of all states.
- Tejinder Pal, in charge of Planning Committee, NGTO expresses her concerns that the teachers are not in confidence due to unawareness of their right. The cloud of doubt to be removed.
- the entire team congratulated Mr. Vijay Mahantesh, President of Karnataka state for the record achievements of fastest 100 registered members. Mr. Vijay has endow the credit to his team members. He also introduced three of the active members from NGTO Karnataka.
- He also shared his experience of success and gave the message to work passionately and to be positive. He also highlighted on the requirements of funds in the expansion of the organization.
- senior members Mr.Pankaj Bhalla and Madam Gopal Pandey blessed the entire team to work with patience for progress.
- West Bengal state President Mr. BinayLaha pointed out about the source of funds as an important factor for development of an organization.
- Mr Ravi Sharma suggested that teachers training to be organized for the awareness of the teachers.

- Mr. Sarat Chandra was of the view that even a single call in a day may help increase awareness among teachers about NGTO.
- Mr. HomnathPaudyal highlighted on the concern of teachers due to non disbursement of teachers salary even for the month of March. He also shares on his vision how he is planning to take the organization to every districts of Manipur.

Mr. Birendra Tripathi and Mr. Indranil Banerjee assured of all kinds of co- operations needed.

- Mr. Pankaj Bhalla suggested that the already drafted letter also to be taken to every DEOs for better response.
- Lastly, Mr. Alok Nagar announced about a news portal to be made available very soon. He requested the NEC family to contribute news events and articles.
- The meeting was concluded with the positive note that NGTO has been moving towards the right direction.
- All members agreed to take the organization to every teachers and come up with lots of positive messages till the NEC Meet next Sunday i,e 10th of May 2020.

[19:36, 05/05/2020] History: NGTO (Punjab and Haryana) Meeting

Minutes of Meeting:

D.O.M : 05.05.2020

Agenda :

1. Planning for spreading activities of NGTO in Punjab and Haryana

2. Appointment of Incharges at Dist. Level
3. Procedure to be followed for the redressal of teachers grievances

Participants:

1. Mr. Virender Nagar (National Co- Ordinator),
2. Mr. BinayLaha (National Spokes person),
3. Mrs. Tajinder Pal Kaur (President Punjab and Haryana)
4. Mr Pankaj Bhalla (Member NEC),
5. Mr. Jagdev Singh (Member NEC)
6. Mr. Rajinder Monga (Member NEC)

The meeting started with the introduction of New NCE members Mr. Jagdev Singh and Mr. Rajinder Monga

-- Mr. Virender Nagar and Mr. Binay suggested some strategies to spread activities of NGTO and highlighted the activities of NGTO in social media and Press media.

--- All the members agreed. Mrs Tajinder Pal Kaur gave suggestion to arrange the meeting of core committee members of Punjab and Haryana on every Friday at 5: 30 PM to discuss the future plans for the upliftment of NGTO in Punjab and Haryana and gave stress on the issue of the promotion of NGTO through print and electronic media.

--- Mr. Jagdev Singh suggested strategy to give vast publicity through facebook etc.

--- Mr. Virender Nagar and Mr. Binoy gave emphasis to appoint incharges at district level and they also explained the process to be followed for the redressal of grievance of any registered member which he/she face at work place

--- The meeting was concluded with the positive note and all members agreed to take the Organization to every teacher even at block level.

[19:36, 8/30/2021] History: Minutes of meeting - NGTO North-East.

Dated : 05-05-2020

Time : 4 pm.

Today, at 4 pm. We had a meeting through Zoom, where following members attended the same :

1. Shri V.K. Nagar
2. Shri BinayLaha
3. Shri H. Paudyal
4. Shri K. Sarkar
5. Shi Joseph
6. One member from Lakhimpur, Assam and Myself.

Members in the meeting, emphasised on following points :

1. NGTO should be constituted at District level.
2. Get the membership increased by choice.
3. Aims and objectives of organisation should be briefly elaborated among teachers.
4. Media cell should be constituted at state level to propogate our existence in print and electronic media.

At last, V.K. Nagar sir suggested with possitve

note to get strengthen our organisation in North-Eastern states by our possitve effort.

Thank you

Rajiv Ranjan Sharma

[19:36, 8/30/2021] History: NGTO (Punjab and Haryana) Meeting

Minutes of Meeting:

D.O.M : 08.05.2020

Agenda :

1. Planning for spreading activities of NGTO in other academic institutions like Pvt colleges along with private schools
2. Procedure to be followed by the State President for redressal of teachers grievances
3. More emphasis to motivate educators to join NGTO
4. Future plans for upliftment of NGTO

Participants:

1. Mr. Virender Nagar (National Co-Ordinator),
2. Mr. BinayLaha (National Spokes person),
3. Mrs. Tajinder Pal Kaur (President Punjab and Haryana)
4. Mr Pankaj Bhalla (Member NEC),
5. Mr. Jagdev Singh (Member NEC)
6. Mr. Ravi (Member NEC)

The meeting started with the action taken by NGTO during last week by making representation to PMO regarding the salary issue

-- Mr. Virender Nagar and Mr. Binay suggested some strategies to spread activities of NGTO and highlighted the activities of NGTO in social media and Press media.

-- Nagar Sir and Binay Sir suggested some measures and procedure to be adopted byState President to redress the grievances of State Board/ CBSE / ICSE board teachers.

--- Jagdev Sir and Tajinder mam highlighted the various irregularities prevailing in institutions as well as the tactics used by the management to exploit the teachers particularly in present scenario.

--- Nagar Sir and Binay sir gave stress that we should remain united at one platform (NGTO); we will raise all the issues at various platforms.

--- All the members agreed. Mrs Tajinder Pal Kaur gave suggestion to arrange the meeting of core committee members of Punjab and Haryana on every Friday at 5: 30 PM to discuss the future plans for the upliftment of NGTO in Punjab and Haryana and gave stress on the issue of the promotion of NGTO through print and electronic media.

--- Mr. Virender Nagar and Mr. Binoy gave emphasis to appoint incharges at district level

--- The meeting was concluded with the positive note and all members agreed to discuss these issues in Sunday meeting of NEC.

[19:37, 8/30/2021] History: NGTO (Punjab and Haryana) General Meeting

Minutes of Meeting:

D.O.M : 09. 05.2020

Agenda :

1. Introduction of New members those have joined NGTO (Pb& Haryana group)
2. Information regarding Aims and Objectives of NGTO to new members
3. Planning for spreading activities of NGTO in Punjab and Haryana

Participants:

1. Mr. Virender Nagar (National Co- Ordinator),
2. Mr. Binay Laha (National Spokes person),
3. Mrs. Tajinder Pal Kaur (President Punjab and Haryana)
4. Mr Pankaj Bhalla (Member NEC)
5. Mr. Jagdev Singh (Member NEC)

The meeting started with the introduction of New members Mr. Sameer Paul, Mr. Kuldeep Singh Virk, Mr. Ravinder, Mrs. Charapreet Kaur, Mr. Manish Malik, Mrs. Mamta Sharma, Mrs. B. Bhattacharya.

-- Binay sir and Varinder Nagar sir explained the Aims and Objectives of NGTO and the future planning of NGTO to all the members

--- Mr. Sameer, Mr. Kuldeep Virk, Mrs. CharanpreetKaur, Mrs. Mamta Sharma and Mrs. B. Bhattacharya put their views regarding the problem they are facing and gave their valuable suggestions.

---- Mrs. Tajinder Kaur and Mr. Jagdev Singh also put forward their point of view on certain problems.

---- Mr. Pankaj Bhalla suggested that maximum teachers should be motivated to register their problems regarding salary and suggestions on face book account or twitter handle of Hon'ble MHRD minister for webinar to be held on 14 May 2020 at 12 noom

--- Mr. Virender Nagar and Mr. Binay gave emphasis to appoint incharges at district level and allocate them their duties

--- The meeting was concluded with the positive note and all members agreed to take the Organization to every teacher even at block level.

[19:37, 8/30/2021] History: Topic: NEC meet

Time: May 24, 2020 12:00 PM

Join Zoom Meeting

https://us02web.zoom.us/j/85761839641?pwd=OE4wYnNJWXN6akNMNVBVNUhTNGI2dz09

Meeting ID: 857 6183 9641

Password: 248982

NEC Meeting agenda

Time duration 1 hour 40 minutes

1. Meeting host by Dr. Birendra Tripathi and Dr. Smriti Sharma.
2. Minutes of meeting by Mr. Indranil Banerji, Dr. Sunita Singh
3. Review and report of last meeting.

4. Announcement and new member introduction, Organizational structural working. Mr. V. K. Nagar
5. Working & Planing, Mr. Sanjay Sharma
6. Importance and use of social media. Mr. Binay Laha
7. Expenses & about Funding of NGTO, Mr. Alok Nagar, Dr. BirendraTripathi/Mr. Indranil Benarji
8. About live Online program by. Anupama Das Program coordinator

End????????????

[19:38, 8/30/2021] History: National Non Government Teachers Organization (NGTO)

Minutes of Meeting

NGTO North East Zone

Dated : the 26th of May 2020

Time : 04: 00 PM

Moderator/Host: Mr. HomnathPaudyal

Convener and State incharge Manipur

Co-Host : Mr. Kartik Sarkar

Incharge NGTO Assam

The agenda of the meeting were introduced. Mr. V. K Nagar, the National President NGTO announced that NGTO Members and State Incharges need to propose a suitable place for a state office in a convenient city. He added that there shall be NGTO offices in every states.

Two new members were introduced to the team. Mr. Ganesh Chhetry represented Noney District, Manipur and Mr. Janak Paudyal represented Imphal

West District Manipur. Mr. Minthang attended the meeting from CCPUR District Manipur. Mr. Chakraborti attended the meeting from Dibrugarh Assam. There were other new members from all over North East but could not be introduced due to internet issue.

National Coordinator, replying to a question related to issuing of identity card to NGTO Members, said that it will be provided in the near future but for time being Authority letters will be issued.

Mr. Rajiv Ranjan Sharma shared his vision for expansion of the organization to every states in North East. He inform the members that NGTO Arunachal Pradesh is already established. NGTO North East is also in contact with two private universities of Assam where their response was positive said the North East incharge.

Mr. Kartik Sarkar, the Assam incharge was positive about the growth of the organization. He inform the members when he was presenting his report on the latest developments of NGTO Assam.

The National Spokesperson Mr. Binay Laha said posting in our own FB timeline and tagging friends help in bringing awareness among others. He added that use of social media would certainly solve the problem of distance. He elaborated with an example saying Mr.Paudyal could organized his team from 2000 km away from the state where he volunteered to be the state incharge.

Mr. Saroj Kumar Sarkar share the challenges that members may come across working in North Eastern region. He shared his wonderful experiences staying more than 20 years in Guwahati and nearby areas. He assured the team of all possible help.

The Host and Convener to Manipur, Mr. Paudyal appreciated all the new members who joined the meeting. He requested the members to encouraged fellow teachers to join for the good cause.

Mr. Ganesh Chhetry applauded the founders and all executives for the initiative that has been taken to bring an organization which stands for private school teachers for the first time. He added that newspaper and Television advertisements can be very useful for general Awareness.

The meeting winded up with the promise to meet next week with more teachers from North Eastern region.

Drafted by

H. Paudyal

[19:39, 8/30/2021] History: Minutes of Eastern zone NGTO meeting

Date :27.05.2020

Host :Samidh Biswas, BinayLaha

State participated: Orissa, West Bengal, Bihar Jharkhand.

The zoom meeting of NGTO's eastern zone was started sharp at 5.30 pm. More than 20 members have taken part. The meeting was initiated Mr Virendra Nagar, the national Co -ordinator and continued by Mr BinayLaha, the in charge of Eastern Zone. Mr Samidh Biswas has focussed on how to make Ngto family a stronger one. Mr Saroj Sarkar, the general secretary of West Bengal has explained the vision of Ngto to every new members. In the mid of his talk Mr virendrapandey has included his concept of making district level more viable for operation so as to get more members. Mr Virendra Pandey from Jharkhand was of the opinion to support the fund through membership. On the other hand Mr Sunil kumar Lima of Orissa focussed on how we can give as best as possible to NGTO. The South Zone NgTO head Mr Vijay Hosur sir gave his notion of strategic plan to go ground level talk for rapid number of membership. Dr Anshul Nigam of Amity University Mumbai has given much importance of labour laws to be included to all non government teachers in India. Mr Jagganath Prasad of Jharkhand has commented upon few important possibilities.Pratima Das madam and Subhra Banerjee madam of Raniganj, West Bengal introduced themselves in this meeting. Mr Palas Naiya, the in charge of Kolkata and South Chabbis Pargana has put his valuable messages through messaging only as network was very slow there for Amphan. Mr Sudeb from Madhya pradesh has kept his valuable messages for NGTO. Dr Sunita Singh has nicely elaborated the point of adding members to the right whatsapp group from different parts of India. Binay Laha has opinionated the same as he also mentioned that he also adds members to the right destination. Mr Navneet Singh has been vocal for the growth of this organization. Mr Mithunghosh, the state president of Bihar has shared his wonderful opinion through messages only as network was slow there. Mr B. N. Prasad, the state in charge of Jharkhand has thoroughly discussed about how he can give a good team in Jharkhand. In the meantime the host Mr BinayLaha was asking Mr Pravin Rajgadia to introduce and to say something about his experience but Mr Pravin Rajgodia ignored to speak. It has been known that he is an owner of a school who took part to know what is all about NGTO. Lastly

Mr Virendra Nagar, the national Co ordinator has rightly explained and answer the questions came from Mr Vijay of Jharkhand. Finally Mr BinayLaha thanked each and everyone for joining this meeting. He keeps the messages to everyone to work unitedly for the betterment of the Non government teachers in India. The presence of Mr Alok Nagar has been another boost up for all the members of this meeting.

Drafted by

Binay Laha

NGTO FAMILY

[19:39, 8/30/2021] History: Minute:

A meeting was organised in Jharkhand NGTO yesterday on 21.06.20 at 8:00 pm in Google meet app. This was the second meeting of NGTO Jharkhand. Meeting was hosted by me in kind presence of our guest Mr. BinayLaha sir, Incharge of Eastern Zone. In this meeting our learned teachers Mr. Sanjay Tiwary, Veerendra Kr. Pandey and Mr. Sarveshwar Singh along with 8 other renowned teachers from Ramgarh and Ranchi. Mr. Sanjay Tiwary sir selected as a Presedent of Ramgarh district. In this meeting we discussed to join more and more members in NGTO Jharkhand. Mr. V.K. Pandey and Mr. Sarveshwar Singh are very active and they will also givensuitable responsibility in near future. All members ensured for their positive support and do for the development of this organisation. It is decided to organise a meeting atleast once in a week and the presence of our national dignitaries is compulsory.

Regards

B. N. Prasad

[19:40, 8/30/2021] History: NGTO NEC Meeting.

Dated: 12th Jul 2020 Sunday

Minutes of Meeting.

H. Paudyal

Host by Mrs.Tajinder Pal Kaur

(President Punjab & Haryana)

NEC Meeting Agenda

1. PIL in High Court and Supreme Court.
2. Scheduling delegation to meet CM.
3. Grievance Redressal Committee.
4. Formation of state / district committees
5. Lifetime General membership

Like the other Sundays, National Executive Committee Members attended the online meeting at 2:00 pm.

The following points were discussed thoroughly with reference to the decided agenda.

1. PIL in High Court or Supreme Court: observing the previous status of one similar PIL in Supreme Court as it was directed to the high court, NGTO decided to move to the high court instead of supreme court for the redressal of private school teachers plight. Where and when will be decided by the NEC latter on.

2. Scheduling delegation to meet CM: NEC discusses that the respective state head should decide the deligate. There should be maximum members. Press conference should be held. The expenses and fares should be voluntarily born by the participants.

3. Grievance Redressal Committee: A new committee is form to address the grievances of teachers. The

committee will be functional under the guidance of National President Mr. Punkaj Bhalla.

The following are the members in the committee

1. Mr. Indranil Banerjee
2. Mr. Sirshendu Chakraborty
3. Mr. Neeraj Makwana
4. Ms. Smriti Sharma.

And one member to be added from NGTO Karnataka.

4. Formation of state / district committees : The respective state's head has brief the session with the progress in committee formation.

Some members volunteer to work for their nearby states. Every NEC member is expected to take-up extra responsibilities in expansion of the organization.

5. Lifetime general membership: NEC has decided that Rs. 1100/ Payment option will be there for lifetime general membership. However the present general membership Rs. 120/ normal renewable option also will be continued.

6. Zero hour: New NEC members were introduced. Some of them were:

1. Dr. Bidyut Saha from Lucknow
2. Mr. Arindam Khamrui from West Bengal
3. Mr. Arpan Shastri from Chhatisgarh
4. Mr. Thang Benjoy from Manipur.

Besides, many issues were brought up for discussion during zero hour. Dr.BidyutSaha and Mr. Thang Benjoy volunteer to help expand the organization to Maharashtra and Tamil Nadu. Mr. Indranil sir volunteer to guide Chhatisgarh. District presidents should also volunteer to help the nearby districts in their respective capacity.

The meeting ended with a vote of thanks by Mr. Jagdishvar Birader from Karnataka.

[19:41, 8/30/2021] History: Thank you all members for joining today's meeting.

Minutes of today's Bengal NGTO Meeting :

Date : 13 July 2020

Participants :

Arindam Khamrui

Amit Paik
Partho Chowdhury
Koushik sinha
Julfikar Khan
Raju Sir
Parimal Das
Pratima Das
Ujjal Sarkar
Indrani Sarkar
Pralay Mukherjee
Oindrila Mukherjee
ParthaPratim Das
Shuvendu Pandit
Mithun Ghosh
Uttam Kumar Das
Saroj Sarkar
Binay Laha

&others

Discussion : Office establishment, Felicitations to the topper students, Proposal for B. Ed colleges south Bengal In charge to Arindam Khamarui and Central Bengal B. Ed colleges in charges to Dr Pradip Kumar Giri (?), and District in charge of Birbhum or Murshidabad to Partha Pratim Das. Security of teachers, No termination movement and salary as per norms.

Vote of thanks : Sarojkumar Sarkar.

Minutes drafted by

Binay Laha

State president of West Bengal

NGTO.

[19:41, 8/30/2021] History: Date :17th July, 2020

Ngto Minutes

NGTO Kolkata

Hoisted by -Paramita Chowdhury

Topic : Kolkata Ngto and it's strategy

Name of the participants :

Indranil Banerjee (State President of NGTO Madhya Pradesh)

Binay Laha (National spokesperson. & State President of West Bengal)

Rajib Ghosh Roy (General secretary of West Bengal)

Paramita Chowdhury (In charge of Kolkata school wings)

Pratima Das (In charge of Raniganj)

Partha Sarathi Das (Executive member of West Bengal)

Palash Naiya (In charge of B. Ed & D. L. Ed colleges, kolkata & South Chabbis Paragana)

Souvik Basu (General Member)

Subhra Banerjee (General Member)

Debabrata Pan (General Member)
Anjan Bera (General member)
& Many others
Vote of thanks: Paramita Chowdhury
Regards
Binay Laha
NGTO Family
Visit www.ngto.in
Mobile 9564926834
[19:42, 8/30/2021] History: NGTO INDIA

NEC Meeting

Dated 26 July 2020 Sunday

Time : 2:00 to 4:00 pm

Minutes of Meeting

Hosted by Dr Sunita Singh State President of Rajasthan

NEC : Meeting Agenda

1. New Members Introduction
2. State Wise Updates
3. Zero session
4. Information.

1. Dr. Sudhir Prasad from Chhattisgarh was introduced as State President.

2. Manpreet Singh State secretary from Uttarakhand.

Statewise Reports

Karnataka : Vijay sir and his team making more members and planning for dharna soon. Target to minimise the teachers problems.

West Bengal and Bihar. Binay Laha and his team doing and did wonderful job by demonstrating with banners, making in social media highlights. Appeals to Private College for Salary updation.

Haryana and Punjab : Tajinder Pal Kaur Mam and team doing excellent performance by doing regular meeting and solving some of the issues under guidance of Pankaj Bhalla sir.

Manipur : State President H Paudyal and Vice President Thang Benjoy doing wonderful work. First time physical meeting conducted in Chandpur district and Benjoy sir started Online and offline teaching for Needyones.

Maharashtra : Under Guidance of Dr Bidyut and Benjoy 6 teachers started on and offline teaching to needy ones and solved rent problems of 2 private teachers.

Uttar Pradesh : Under Guidance of Dr Tripathi and Madan Pandey sir made district incharges in several places. ASHUTOSH SHARMA contributed 21000 from Bareilly and Dr Bidyut solved 3 cases related salary in Lucknow, management will not sack any teacher. Tree plantation was done in Aashiana police station.

Other states also make valuable contribution towards enrichment of NGTO.

Zero session : Discussed related PM letter and further procedure and teachers in problems must give complain to concern state.

Icon of NGTO V Nagar sir told about regular presence and grievance redressal. Vijay sir and team will be reporting and meeting soon under the impression of Experience Pankaj Bhalla sir.

Tulsi Dubey sir told about starting of Chankaya Magazine articles in hindi and Laha sir taking incharge for English version.

Alok Nagar Sir requested to submit email and photo.

Information : Tajinder Pal Kaur and Vijay sir, Dr Smriti discussed general issues along with all. Kamlesh Sharma, Chakraborty sir, Ghosh sir, Arpan Sastri sir and all involved to make stronger and fight together. Manpreet Singh team will do good in Uttrakhand and Bidar express valuable points.

It was around 22 members attended and well managed and mannered by Dr Sunita Singh and vote of thanks by Binay Laha acting as actual PRO.

Writer

Dr Bidyut and M Pandey.

[19:27, 8/30/2021] History.

3

Suffering of a Termination in a Private School and the Partial Collapse of Education in India

Today I am going to write few words on Termination and the collapse of partial education in the private schools in India. This practice of termination is not new to a private school. It existed in the colonial period and after the Independence of India. We have got political freedom from the British, still we are not free to our will and work. Teaching has been labelled one of the most noble profession of the world. So is for India, too. But in India, teaching has been divided in basically two parts so far as the sector is concerned. One is teaching in a government sector and teaching in a private sector. As I started my carrier as a private school teacher decades ago I am having a fair and rough experience in this field. I have seen teachers of the both sectors closely. The politics and facilities of the teachers in the government sector has seen many ray of hope since the beginning of the twenty first century once the pay commission introduced to them bulk. I can remember that when I was in my class twelve some words floating from the teachers staff room that the teachers are now happy as they are paid more than enough. This was around twelve thousand in 2000 at the time of joining, or little bit more or less. Exact data has not been collected. I can also remember that my elder uncle in whose quarter I started to gain much prominence of my consciousness as a student used to get nearly nine thousand of salary as a senior technical attendant at Durgapur Steel plant. Nine thousand in a month was not too good but it was moderate to run a mediocre family. The status of a government school teacher changes rapidly in the beginning of the twenty first century. I hope, if I am not wrong, this was the picture of entire India. This is matter of pride that government ensures the security of the jobs of teachers in her sectors and other government employees till retirement and even after retirement in the means of a lucrative pension to his or her better half after their death, rarity of this situation happens in case of typical awkward situation or extreme complex lacunae.

Termination of a teacher in a private school :

This is a matter of surprise and common normalcy that you may not have chance to continue your teaching if you have small silly mistake like attending the class little late than time, subtle clashes with management or with principal or with a tiny misbehaviour with students. You don't have any right to put a question to the system. But it doesn't mean that no one questions. Those who question against a system in a private school must have to face many hurdles. Actually they will be alineated from the system. Their names will be withdrawn from different committes, they will be given extreme class pressure or they will given no classes at all. Worry to add that you won't be given place to the school magazine or to the cultural committe and you will remain a forever deprive soul. A close eye will be watching from all corners to him or her. You can understand what will happen next. Probably you will low increment years after years. Will you be a able to survive in this situation?

Personal experience on Termination :

I used to get only 2500 rupees per month as a salary as an assistant teacher in a private school in Durgapur, West Bengal in 2008. The school I have joined was not popular and not affiliated too. The management was trying their level best to get it affiliated. I wish to add that the management have been able to create reputation for promoting education. But the inside story was totally dark. Interestingly this school was having only two male teachers. One was the clerk cum teacher and the another one is the writer himself.This school was growing rapidly with the particular sentiment of the patrons of the school. Indeedteachers in a private school have no pivotal role in making policy. In government a good politician may try to upgrade the system and can be done with the consultation of the headmaster along with the teachers. Manish Sisodia, the present education minister of Delhi Government and the Deputy Chief Minister wrote in his book Shiksha - "I have visited a school at Patparganj village the day after swearing in as the education minister of Delhi. This was my first surprise inspection. "(1)page 123, Shiksha. Later on he added his experience -"I found the doors and windows broken, fans broken, and electrical wires dangling. I asked the principal of that school, to which he replied, sir as you know, most of the students come out from the slums out back. They spoil everything "(2,page no 123, Shiksha). After watching this terrible conditions of the government schools Manish Sisodia took the challenge to transform the attitude and the education system in the government schools. He further added, "My first challenge was to present a blueprint for future plans to all my officers, from senior ones in the education department to those at the district and zonal level. (3, page no 124-125, Shiksha). So he was successful in transforming the education system in the government schools in Delhi. But at the same time he never felt to upgrade the financial status of the teachers in the private schools in Delhi. Teachers in the private schools may get better salary than the rest of the country but not all the private schools do not care for it in Delhi. Many of the private school teachers in Delhi have been terminated in Delhi during lock down period. They have lodged complains to the teachers organisation but it goes futile as the central machineries are in the hand of the government. The transformation of the government schools in Delhi by Manish Sisodia is highly political to gain vote bank but he ignored it to mention it as political. However his intention to transform can not be ignored, it deserves to be praised because twenty five percent of Budget money have been allocated to education sector in Delhi during Arvind Kejriwal's rule. This is highest ever investment from a state government for this this sector in comparison to any other states in India. My point of focus was the worth mentioning role of the policy makers, in private sector it is the management. So automatically The teachers feel ignored while the utility of their teaching is taken but separated to make any policy. Actually Private sector schools in India follow the exam pattern circulated by the board, the others are highly individual and it varies mercilessly from one school to another. However I left my first school in a sense of dissatisfaction in regard to salary and role of a teacher. I was not terminated there but I failed to survive there. But I have seen others to leave that school due to the same problems I have faced. I did not have an appointment letter there so I felt no need to resign. Actually this is the saddest part of maximum private school teachers in India that they are not issued appointment letter at the same of their joining which I consider to be mostly illegal. Teachers don't demand it as they know that they may loose their jobs if they demand it. Many number of Principles do not have appointment letter and their original certificates the management keep in their custody to play a dirty game.This is painfully illegal and heinous crime to snatch the original certificates of the principals and the teachers. I have seen many principals to be terminated without any reason. Everything depends on the master will of the management. I have once been terminated in a semi religious English medium schools as I have demanded my appointment letters. As in consequence, I was threatened to leave town in which I am living now. They were faulty, idiot and illegal and illiterate but they were making me faulty because I demanded my Appointment letter which is my right. I don't think that I have done any mistakes. Actually I tried to speak for others also. But speaking for others may curtail you from jobs which I felt I have been alienated by other teachers also. There is a Bengali proverb, *Jar jonnyo churi Koro, sei bole tumi chor* literally it means for whom you steal will call you a thief. I felt such. Internally few teachers supported me but they wanted fruits without planting the tree as they were hopeless for years. Later on I joined another big school in Bihar. But I have not forgotten to issue a legal notice to the former school. This was because of me no teachers have been terminated in the last eight years. At the same time I remain crititical in my writing in the newspaper either in the form of letters or in the post editorial page. Few government employee they don't not care for arrival to their office, they sat hours after hours to the private school I have worked. This is pathetic to listen to him while he talks of idealism and teaching method. It is the corruption of the government institution that they don't take care of their staffs or don't suspend them from Primary council while they invest maximum time in a private school as an unofficial managent members to get a whooping respect from teachers, shamelessly.

Less salary is not a factor but the private school teachers need security of their jobs for the greater good of education in India. India promotes fifty percent of school school education through private schools but ninty five percent private schools do not follow the norms of salary or the norms of termination. Verbal termination is the end of all suggestions. It is just like a fight in between an elephant and a goat and just like a capitalist and an orphan. Might is right every where. The capitalist management throws the teachers into the garbage after using them.

Will the good day for private school teachers come in India?

It is not the best salary that may change the pattern of lives of the private school teachers. It is the attitude that has to be changed. The Kothari Commission or the National Education Policy 1986 has shown no such sympathy for the teachers in private schools in India. The sum total growth of education will come up when the teachers, management and the students will act as a single family. Does it happen so? It happens in words, but not in concretisation. I should mention Gurudev Rabindranth Tagore who was anxious to recruit Kshitimohan Sen with all respect. Tagore promised Mr Sen to afford a good amount of salary while Kshitimohan was recruited in Visva Bharati. Quoting AmrtyaSen, the Nobel Laureate, in his" Home in the world on this particular occasion may serve my purpose. It is not the salary but the affection and love and respect of Tagore led Kshitimohan Sen to become a teacher at Santiniketan as he had already been offered a good job in the nearby state. Amartya Sen wrote, "The salaries were very low at Santiniketan School and Kshitimohan had a large family, including not only his own children but also the sons (Biren and Dhiren) of his deceased elder brother Abanimohan. "(4,Page no 65, Home in the world, Amartya Sen) Later on it was added that "Tagore continued his pleading and said that he would make sure that Kshiti Mohan's remuneration would be adequate for him to meet his family obligations" "(5), page no 66, *Home in the World*, Amartya Sen. This is very important of what Tagore supported a teacher. This is the love and faith relationship that may join the broken bond of faithlessness in between teachers and Management. The teachers need security of their jobs from State and Central government. State government should not ignore that the private English medium schools do not under their jurisdiction or the Central government should not say that education is in the concurrent list so state government should interfere it. I wish to add that I have written a letter to the PMO regarding the status of my job. They have done a wonderful thing. They have sent it to the state government education department and then the state government education department has sent it to the District Inspector of Education and then the District Education officer called me to call for a meeting with the school in which I work. But I was aware of the situation. No where I mentioned the name of my present school to understand the actual reality. So if have to sit with my managent for solving the dispute which already I have done I will remain a valueless one. Therefore the concerned higher authorities to whom I have sent my play must act confidentially to solve my problems or the problems of private school teachers in India. Will it happen? The private school education system has crossed many hurdles. Now it has reached to the Capitalist Intervention from the Colonial Care. So the aesthetic and dirty lynching of the Capitalist upon the gentle fearful private school teachers is highly expected, until teachers are soully united. Last but not the least if the atmosphere in a private school is created in such a way that the teachers won't keep a second thought to join a government school or any other financial reputation. The support and Co operation from both government is highly required to change the suffering of a private school teacher into love so that they can propagate better love and humanism among the students, the soul business tool of the management.To resist the partial collapse of education the termination must have to be stopped. If a pigeon is given crops on our roof, it will come with a hope but if the pigeon is driven out with a nasty sound, it must not return.

4

Lockdown, Corporatism and Challenges of the Private English Medium School Teachers in India

Covid -19 has enraptured the entire world since the beginning of 2020.As in consequence the first lock down was declared in Hubei province in China in the month of January 2020.Next was in İtaly in the month of March 2020.India has also declared nation wide lock down from 24 march 2020.Nearly 63 countries of the World declared lock down for safety as it was proven Spanish flu in the year 1914 onwards that lock down is really the best to safeguard ourselves. Covid -19 has hit the global education system for a long period of time which is not still without problems. While this researcher is trying to shape up this article, he is not without the fear of corona. Today is 24 th of August 2021 but the news related to corona and the fear of third wave is continuing to be a subject of prolong seriousness as many scientists are in fear of third wave may sweep the entire India and the world accordingly from the month of October 2021.This is a suspect which should not be ignored as already we are crossing the second wave with all its dangerous consequences. Worry to add that this corona has been successful in killing nearly 40 lakhs people all over the globe. This is largest ever deaths the world has ever witnessed.

Death of many celebrities in India :

Corona has killed many famous people in India. The famous media person Rohit Sardana died. His pathetic appeal for Ramdesivir medicine has shook the medical crisis. Despite of Government's hard attempt we failed to save lakhs of lives. We have lost Soumitra Chatterjee, the icon of Indian film, specially Bengali cinema in corona. Eminent poet and Critic Sankha Ghosh went to heavenly abode. Anjan Bandhopadhaya, the brother of Chief Advisor to Chief Minister of West Bengal and the chief Editor of Zee Bangla News left us. The list of death due to corona is too long.

Death of Private school teachers due to Corona :

India is a vast country. It is quite difficult to collect the data of the death of the teachers in private schools. But through newspaper and through television channels we have come to know death of many private school teachers. Even it was news that a private school teacher from bihar committed suicide due to the excessive crisis of money as she lost her job during lock down.

Lockdown and Corporatism and Challenges of the Private English medium schools teachers :

Corporatism has been a common practice of the owner of the private schools in India despite their behaviarial attempt and professionalism to carry it. Corporatism does not actually means a sadistic pleasure comes out of execution of the management, rather it is such a process through which the should be undisturbed from both end. Mere chalk and Duster method of application in the field of teaching has become outdated, added to it the digital board or smart board or using laptop in the classroom or any latest technology has been adopted for the progress of education as well as for running the education business very smoothly. What exactly attracts the patrons of the private English medium schools is the smartness of the dress code of the students, teachers and all non-teaching staffs also. Fluency in English, digitalisation of class or copying the latest foreign model of education helps patrons to invest money for the future of their children. This is partly illusion and partly true as the entire government schooling sector failed to draw the students from the economically sober classes. This is indeed a fact that the conditions of the government schools except Delhi has fallen to the sediment. Every one will agree to that. The basic ignorance to promote English education in the government schools is another dead factors to get admission in the private English medium schools.

Who teaches in the private English medium schools? Are they excellent?

A recent study shows that nearly fifty percent students read in the private schools. The numbers of the students may be few crores and the teachers are also nearly crore, this is an assumption as government does not have exact data of all the affiliated and the non affiliated private schools. Private schools in India are predominantly English medium schools, which is without doubt. The process of recruitment in the private English medium schools vary from one school to another. Some branded schools recruit the teachers through written test and Viva. Some schools do not follow any pattern. Some schools follow open viva system of recruitment through newspaper advertisement. And in most of the cases teachers are recruited through proper channels. Similarly the salary of the teachers differ from school to school. Nearly and roughly five percent schools pay as per norms or they pay more than this as per the demand or bargaining of the teachers. And the rest ninty five percent schools do not offer not more than fifteen thousand rupees per month.This is a sad point to note that many scholars force teacher to sign in registers in a complete different salary package being not offered to them for ever. No cbse officers, icse officers or the District inspector of school have investigated this hemlock situation doggedly or it may be that they know everything and pretend to know nothing at all else their inability to resist it will turn into vain to the capitalist venture. In this fearful situation the best teachers prefer to leave the school and tries a find a job in the said five percent schools.It has been observed that few teachers from a reputed school in kishanganj District, Bihar, left their teaching and started up a new small business like opening up clothes store, or setting up a hotel business. They have opined that they left for the management has broken their promises to yearly increment which is really meagre. And they lead a better peaceful life than their job of teaching. Now in this situation merit is obstructed to better finance and mental stability. A typical trend of minds always prefer to become a teacher and it is heard that teaching is the last profession to choose. I have been bullied several times by many teachers of why I have chosen to be a private school teacher in a distant land like kishanganj which is nearly

500 kilometers away from my home town Durgapur. Actually people can't think to move for a better haven in this field. But it is a very regular picture that the teachers oftentimes change their place of Job due various crisis. I should not forget to add the point of local teachers and non local teachers. The non locals are always paid better salary than the local teachers. This tradition is going on since independence. It is worth remembering that geyojogivikh pay Na which means a village saint do not get alms easily. On the other hand local teachers are engaged in tuition manipulation and they sometimes earn huge money out of manipulation. Actually this is an art to have maximum tuitions without teaching better but exceptional things do also happens. I have seen many wonderful local teachers who are dedicated and non manipulative, yet they get good number of tuitions. So the teachers who teaches in the English medium schools are mixed in quality and experience. I can not say that they are always best but I can assure that they are much better than the government school teachers whose mentality, attitude and culture is as sluggish as an old clever men who passes only tricks to manage the situation. Government teachers are actually god gifted.

Technological expertisation mandatory in a private school :

During lock down many pictures have been viral. We have seen students to make mockery upon teachers inability to teach in front of the camera. The smart phone usage and the usage of laptop have become a compulsory medium to communicate work from home. As there were no other ways rather than adopting this system, as this is not a government system in which teachers are paid without teaching for more than than a year, the private management have kept all roads open to continue their business in different struggle and method to anyhow satisfy the patrons and the students of the schools. Day and night teachers worked hard in preparing the lessons and making videos of their teaching. Recording the teaching and sharing among the students through whatsapp group was another resistance. Teaching through You tube channel has become very common in differnt parts of India. The use of various soft ware remained highly effective. Management do have a responsibility to run the online institutions in a proper way as the awaaz was going on regarding "No schools No fees". Many of the fees have been curtailed during lock down. Many of the teachers have been terminated due to lack of fund and their non performance in the online classes. The teaching has become mostly open and private numbers of the teachers have become universal for 24 hours. Showing the courage and openness of acceptance was mandatory for the teachers in such a situation where education system was supposed to be fallen. Where government system of education has already collapsed but it won't be wrong to add that all government school teachers and all other government employees send their children to the private schools for all round benefits. Lock down was exemplary. The flow of education remained intact in the private schools. Completion of syllabus, organising the periodical test all have been regular due to the labour of the teachers. They deserve a big thank which they get very rarely. It is like use and throw game which I have observed personally.

Hope is the ultimate solution :

We can not but hope always for the good days to come. The situation of the government school teachers have gone through changes after many struggles and revolution. They have gone to the court to understand their rights. The process has just began in private sectors. One day the attitude towards private school teachers will change. They will not be terminated without any sufficient reasons. They don't have to face much difficulties which they don't deserve. This is the sum total system which needs to be changed. Teachers, I hope, will get salary as per norms of the government as a huge number of private school teachers are conjectured to be their vote bank. I have mentioned it as nothing good changes will happen until you are turned to be a vote bank. Good days are sure to come.

5

Private Vernacular Schools in India and Its Present Situation

There is no substitute of mother tongue. The best was to learn is to get the knowledge through mother tongue. Rabindranath Tagore, the first Asian Nobel laureate, told that mother tongue is just like mother's milk. He writes on its essentiality. No one can ignore the neccesity to learn and cultivate mother tongue. India is a multilingual country since its inception. There are more than thousand languages in India in which 22 languages are mostly important language as per eight schedule of Indian Constitution. Apart from these 22 languages in the eight schedule Hindi and English both play a pivotal role in the central government government works. The state governments do have their different priorities. In the non Hindi speaking states the major languages of their are prominent like Bengali in west Bengal, Marathi in Maharashtra, Tamil in Tamilnadu or Assamese in Assam.

Private Vernacular Schools in India :

In India private vernacular schools are affiliated to the state board or few are run by Central Board of

Secondary Education. In comparison to English medium schools the vernacular schools are less in number so far as the demand of the English medium schools are concerned. Specially to add that the vernacular private schools are limited to the primary level. On the other hand maximum number of vernacular schools are governed by the state government. Indeed India is having maximum number of government vernacular schools which may surpass the number of private English medium schools in India. The setting up of private vernacular schools reminds us of the language sentiment and the indifference of the government run vernacular schools. Patrons always want care to their wards in the schools even at the cost of investing money. They always want a better education for their children which they lack in the government schools. But at the same time they want modern education with all its facilities. Many trustees do establish vernacular schools for their own agenda. Privatisation of education is indeed the irresponsibility of government to promote holistic education. There are some religious and political interest laid down to promote education through vernacular medium. Schools are best platform to socialise and to promote the culture as per the interest of the trustees. Many religious trustees right from Hindu, Muslim, Sikhs, Christians to Jains run their own schools in India. Rastriya Swayam Sevak Sangha is one of such bigesst trust that runs no less than forty thousand vernacular schools including English medium schools through out India. Many Muslim trusts also are running hundreds of vernacular schools. We can not ignore the religious link to language link in those schools. Privatisation in schools in India is no longer a secular one. During colonial times many private schools were governed by the christians missionaries. It won't be a mistake if I add that many number of vernacular schools are governed by Christian missionaries apart from running private English medium schools.

Are the Vernacular Private Schools in Demand?

This is a very relative thing to describe whether the vernacular private schools are having craze. It has been observed that in many places people are preferring to send their children to the vernacular private schools despite of the presence of many English medium schools or many government schools. This always depends on the performance and track record of the school. I wish to mention the name of a school in Durgapur in the Paschim Bardhaman district. The school is still running with all her pride with little campus but always having excellent results. This Bidhan Chandra institution, I can remember, in her nostalgia flight was having only one storey building with asbestos. But the students from all over the town jumped to take admission there. The results were excellent. All used to get star marks, I mean more than 75 marks which was a matter of pride for every student to score such marks. We may include the vernacular private schools of the Ramakrishna mission though out India for their outstanding performance to cultivate meritorious students years after years. So it completely relative to describe the essentiality of the private vernacular schools. The demands private medium schools may grow rapidly but we can't ignore the role of the private vernacular schools in India.

Salary /Remuneration /Sammanik or Dakhhina of a teacher in the vernacular private schools in India :

Tear shed in my eyes when we are anxious to know the exact data regarding the salary of a teacher in a private vernacular school in India. It starts from 700 rupees per month in the rural India, sometimes increases to 2500 in the semi urban area, and in the urban are it may go to 7000 to 10000(ten thousand maximum).Ninety nine percent schools of this type do provide such a little amount of money that they are bound to have tuitions or remain lazy in the classroom amidst pressure. While I have served as a National Spokesperson I used to get many calls from different parts of India, hearing them crying for their jobs and security and remuneration. I got a call from Uttar Pradesh regarding a teacher who has been slapped by one of the member of the owner group. I got a call from a madam, of Cooch Bihar district of West Bengal, who shares her story that they have been threatened to leave the school. I was quite in a puzzled situation. I asked her salary. It was only 1300 rupees. I could have told simply to leave the school and join other schools but it is a matter of igo that she and her friends were working there for long six years. So I took the risk. I asked the number of the school owner. I call him after few hours and gave hot doses and said that I will complain to the District primary school officer to deaffilate this school as they are terminating two teachers during pandemic. But who will listen to whom? These are two examples I have given. Every day many cases of termination are happening. Teachers are so lessly paid that they can not even afford legal fight. Teachers do not go to the court for social shame. The members of their houses do not support to move to the court in fear that they will never get a second job. I have personally interested to talk to a teacher leader from Gorakhpur, Uttar Pradesh. He runs a teacher's organization to support the private school teachers. He also blows the same opinion that in Gorakhpur if a teacher is terminated he won't get a second job of teaching easily in the same time as the owner of the schools are connected each other. The owner of the private schools share completely false stories to You if you wish to listen why salaries are so less. Very cleverly some schools use the term honorium or sammanik or Dakhinna to cover their fault of giving payment as per norms. I have a bitter experience to talk to a owner of a karnataka based private school. He threatened me directly that I put any enquiries regarding the salary of a teacher in his school. The mentality of the management is worse. The role of the government is mostly worse.

Motivation of Teaching

Teaching is a very respectful profession. Indeed many join in this sector for respect. In Indian ancient society teachers are next to god. But in contemporary society teachers in a vernacular private schools treated as per the choice of the management. This revelation of the pathetic condition of the teachers has deteriorated the teacher student relationship. Teachers are not longer treated as a teacher. They are treated as facilitator. But it was supposed to not to happen. Very recently I was going through Manish Sisodia's book "Shiksha" in which he had elaborated the past and the present status of a teacher. He tried to uplift the status of a teacher in Delhi. He puts the reference on teachers from the ancient text -

"Guru Govind dou Khade

Kake lagun paye?

Balihari guru apne Govind diyo bataye.

It means both god and my teacher stand in front of me, whom do I now to? I am indebted to you, Teacher, for You have shown me the way to god".

The situation and status of a private vernacular school teacher has gone through rapid distortion. Actually no observer has been recruited from the government to scrutinize them when they are hopeless. Central government is making us dream five trillion economy to make India one of the most powerful country of the world. Alas! How can the government ignore their existence? However government is clever enough to reduce the education expenditures by helping to opening up private vernacular schools.

Future of private vernacular schools and her teachers:

I find no bright future for the said category of schools as they failed to meet the financial and social respect to the teachers. Teachers are always the pillars of the schools. But giving them disturbances, the education system can not run smoothly. The schools, if they are hiding their goals in the name of education, may promote any other things or they may do business, but surely not education. The government should stand visionary to guide and support the teachers else it collapes with all her central machineries. Most sensitive part of education The students should not suffer because of the deprivation of the teachers in the private vernacular schools in India in the twenty first century. Hare Krishna.

6

Psychology and Vision of the Management of the Private Schools

Primarily, the psychology and the vision of the management of the private schools are money, respect, commitment and organisational pleasure. More may be added but I have found not more than these. I have been in experience in teaching different schools in different parts of India and I have the pleasure to read in five universities in India. I have taught at Surendra Chandra Modern School (Durgapur), Guru Tegbahadur public school (Durgapur) for few hours, Bethany Mission school (Primary Section at Hemtabad, Uttar Dinajpur District), Sarada Vidya Mandir (Raiganj, Uttar Dinajpur) Green Field Public school (Jammu and Kashmir) Bal Mandir Senior Secondary School (Kishanganj, Bihar) and in Bethany Mission School (Raiganj, West Bengal) including I was qualified to teach in a school in Purnea in Bihar and a school in Delhi and Kolkata. I have been in touch for nearly five hundred private school teachers through out India for organisational works and for my love to them. I have attended nearly two hundred virtual meetings with the teacher leaders and with the head of the organization of the teachers. Got pleasure when I have heard from the Secretary Honorable Nabalkishore Agarwal that I deserve to be the principal of Balmandir Senior Secondary school, a school is having a wonderful reputation with no less than three thousand students. This school was set up in 1973 with only 37 students at her inception. I have the pleasure to deal and watch the management people of different schools as I try always to be a dedicated teacher. While I was in Sarada Vidya Mandir I used to come wearing a white dhoti and white Punjabi in Marathi style as per the tradition of RSS as the school is governed by RSS but affiliated to CBSE, Delhi. I have forgotten to add that I have visited nearly hundred schools in different parts of the country, including many colleges and universities. I have visited nearly all university campuses both government and private in West Bengal, my home state. I have the high pleasure to visit Jawaharlal Nehru University, Benaras Hindu University, PV Narasimha University, Hyderabad, Vasant Kanya Mahavidyalaya etc. Adding more to this venture I have attended nearly two hundred literary festivals in west Bengal and in different universities in India in my twenty one years of literary career. I compose poems in a regular mode and I love to read books of all varieties which interest me. I edit an English Magazine named *Indology* which is considered to be the first English magazine in Uttar Dinajpur District of West Bengal. Now questions may arise of why I am giving my personal ambition and activities and dealing to write down the psychology and vision of the management. My way of living has added extra benefits to me to watch them closely in a transparent vision as already I have faced many troubles and challenges in dealing with the people of India, at large. But I have never become hopeless. I love to stand for all positive vibes that will change the educational atmosphere. My purpose of writing is not to distort the image and prestige of the management as they have the guts to crate job opportunities for millions of teachers in India. Hats off to them as I believe that it is better to give a job rather than doing a job is universally accepted. But more we can expect from them as only 5 percent of the total private schools are following the norms of the government so far as the salary of the teachers are concerned. Many schools managent do not have a clear vision. I have a friend in Balarampur District in Uttar Pradesh. He runs a private school. He told me once that he wants to give a better salary and motivation to his teachers but he can't afford as his school is not affiliated. He had taken a vow that the day the school will get affiliated will disburse as per norms. That is a good thing. He has a clear vision. The same way I wish to mention the the biggest school of world City Montessori school in Lucknow, Uttar Pradesh never compromise with the salary of the teachers. Dr Gandhi has this foundation. He has shown that this is possible. In every newspaper advertisement of his schools keeps the pride to recruit teachers all over the country with highest financial respect. It is a very common thing that many schools keeps on advertising several times in a year regarding their recruitment. What does it mean? Simply it defines that the teachers do not want to stay there for long time. The situation is not stable there. There is a profit if a teacher leaves the school, there is a profit if a teacher joins the school. This has been a common man practices of many schools that they do not pay the teachers through out the year. They terminate teachers verbally before any long vacation. Huge amount of money summed up in the account of the school but it indicates the nasty mentality of the management who thinks only of money.

Respect and commitment of the management :

Respect can not be demanded, it is commanded-heard it from a management people who referred few teachers in a serious meeting that he will never give respect to those teachers who demand respect. At once a madam answered it tactfully to him that it is the upbringing of those children had affected their mind to think to not to give respect all teachers. Respect is a big and comparatively relative matter. I have heard from many teachers that "We don't want respect, we want fifty thousand rupees of salary". They added that we will not let the respect to chew and it day and night. If we don't have money, we don't have respect in the society. I find both the attitude are extreme and painful. Management want respect from teachers but they are not ready to give respect to the teachers. It should be inter mutual and vice versa. The same thing can be plated to the management that they should not demand respect but they should command respect. I will add now a very funny comment of a semi baked good soul of a managent people who used to say, *"Humlog school mey samman ke liye aate hai, samman milega to ayenge, nehi milega to nehi ayenge. Humlog business man hai, utna time nehi hai."* I have met with him personally he is having a wonderful human nature with all frankness and simplicity of his heart. Actually teachers wanted him to come at school regularly as other management people used to frighten the teachers in different ways. Few management I have seen do not keep any promises for the new generation and for the better glory of the world. They love to listen "Sir "everytime and even if it is not passed properly nemesis may come in the form of Termination. *Dekh lenge* attitude should not be entertained at school. Government must scrutinize through proper Channel so that a peace can always prevail at school as the teachers and the management both have to deal with the petals before blossoming.

Organisational pleasure of the management :

This is very important in India. The capitalist, the rich men establish a school apart from their other businesses. This has been a common tendency after operation chalk and duster during Rajib Gandhi Government and later on during Narasima Rao government. Once the liberalisation of economy begins in India in the year 1992 the individuals having monetary back ran for setting up private schools for business, organisational pleasure in the name of education. I will leave few philanthropist businessmen who had truly shown their commitment towards society and nation. But the rest always ran for lucrative gain in their rat's ralley. The exposure of their recognition soon turns to be the organisational pleasure and entertainment so far as their policy is concerned. This attitude needs rapid change and it should be converted to only educational development for the greater good of our society. Mal intention can not be a vision.

7

Old Private School Education System in India

Private school education system in India is old and new at the same time. There is a great rejuvenation of private school system in our country as the parents are afraid to send their children to a government school, if get no other way than sending. And at the same time it was the only system that our Undivided India was having. The system of Pathsala or gurukulam or Acharya kulam is as old as Hindu knowledge and civilisation. Students need to stay at teacher's house years after year till his completion of study. There were no concept of nation or government like today. The education used to be promoted at individual effort. The students need to bear the cost of study at Gurukulam. Teachers had been given highest respect and reason next to god. It was the duty of the students to study only. So was said, ChhatranamAdhyanam Tapa. On the other hand Gurus or teachers were considered to be Brahma, the Hindu deity or Bisnu,the Hindu deity whom Hindu people worship ages after ages.

The pollution of caste started during the later vedic period. Religious study used to be imparted as per profession and caste. The Brahmans students used to get knowledge of Sanskrit, Hindu Scriptures and deities, The khatryias used to knowledge on war, The vaishas on their profession and Shudras were given lesson to their work and often neglected to impart education to them. The education, sometimes used to be patronised by the kings but it was not holistic during ancient times.

After the advent of Islam in India the religious Islamic education had been imparted through maktabs. The study of Koran and Sharia was mandatory there. During the entire Islamic phase the sultanate rulers and the Mughal rulers promoted Islamic studies in India. The Hindu system of education was also running like the same system India had adopted in the ancient times.

In the British period the colonial education, I mean western knowledge and light,had been promoted by the Christians missionaries largely after the 1813 charter Act which allowed them to set up churches and schools in India. The passing of Macaulay minute in 1835 was another landmark decision of the British government to promote English education in India for the Indians to be recruited as an intermediary to the British and at the same time it opens up the job opportunity to the lower level for the educated Indian. Though Asiatic Society of Calcutta under the mentorship of William Jones tried to restore the glory of Indian ancient education through indigenous languages it failed to restrict the choices of Indian elites. The opening up of three Modern Universities in 1857 was another milestone to promote modern education through private schools. As the Christian Missionaries took care of English medium schools and other private schools vernacular languages they remained victorious rather than the other Indian management of education. The major cities of India witnessed and got the benefit of Colonial western education. Calcutta, Bombay, Delhi, Madras were the best advantageous. Hills too also have been given top priority. Darjeeling, Kerseong, Kalimpong, Simla, Dehradun, Shilong, Mussourie and many other hilly towns took the advantage of western knowledge and light. The promotion of Christian religion through setting up missionary schools can not be ignored. Those colonial private schools are still holding their head higher in promoting education apart from capitalist venture to set up chain group of schools nation wide since the proud independence of our motherland.But at the same time the legacy that those colonial schools bear has no match. The best English medium schools of India are in their custody, at least the patrons prefer to think so.

8

Psychology and Innocence of the Students in English Medium Schools

বর্ষেবর্ষেদলেদলে

আসেবিদ্যামঠতলে

চলেযায়তারাকলরবে।

-কালিদাসরায়

Barse Barse dole dole

Ase bidyamothotole

Chole jai tara kalorobe.

Years after years
Years after years
Students come and go
And talk of Michael Angelo.

(This is my aesthetic translation of the above stanza of Kalidas Roy)

One of my former student whose name was forgotten but his surname I can recall was Mukherjee who taked to me over phone while he was crossing Bardhaman Station. He was from Kishanganj Bal Mandir Senior Secondary School. He was telling me over phone that he was missing my teaching and recalling my classroom as already I have left that school and joined a cbse based senior senior secondary school in Raiganj the I place I wished to return to stay with my family. I did not have any other way rather than than coming back to Raiganj as my wife is a pgt teacher at a government school in Uttar Dinajpur District and We have a small kid. The day I heard the Nobel Prize speech of Kailash Satyarthi that Every child is special and every childhood is special. It shook my mind. The other reason to leave that school was my literary venture as I wanted to come back to Bengal to compose and promote literature significantly. Actually I was missing my literary partners in kishanganj. Later on I have acquinted few Bengali writers in Kishanganj and Purnea district. I could have matched my frequency with English writers and Bengali writers, otherwise, there were many Hindi writers who cultivate literature in Kishanganj. I can only speak Hindi as per requirement and read Hindi very slowly with much stress but I can't not write Hindi. I don't get pleasure in reading Hindi newspaper or Hindi books while I have tried to read few. Whatever Hindi I have learnt in my life it was because of the students and teachers of Bal Mandir Senior Secondary school. It was their innocence that they have tolerated my tuta fata hindi in a broken style for nearly two years of my career there. Though I have never spoken Hindi in the class room in the first five years. I have spoken to them outside the school campus or in the school campus after the school is over. But last few months I have broken all norms of my interdisciplinary idealism and vow and started speaking Hindi in the classroom too. Actually Indian school students do prefer bi lingual mode of education for clarity of expression and understanding. Students are always innocent like that

Mukherjee who called me from Bardhaman Station as I belong to Undivided Bardhaman district, basically. My ancestral village Srikrishnapur is situated in the Durgapur Sub Division in the present Paschim Bardhaman District. Now I remind that my upper primary school happened in a private school adjacent to a government primary school where I have completed my primary education. I can not distinguish the care between the teachers of my both primary and upper primary school at my ancestral village. Both schools were fantastic. Teachers were excellent in taking care of the study and sports of the children. We have never disrespected our teachers in those schools. I was personally a favorite boy of my teachers as I was extremely obedient and I stood first from class two to class eight. I have been directly promoted to class two because my teachers found something different within me than the other students. My father was very good hearted to give highest respect to the teachers. Whenever there was any celebration at our home he used to invite all my teachers.But he was not academically bright. He was under matriculated. Education is, actually, the inner pulse of a man, I believe. At the same time I wish to add that we have spent many good things with our teachers apart from the school class room teaching. A teacher by name Subhas Sarkar used to help us in pulling us out from the home and gave his friendly lectures on the bank of Tumuni River while it used to get flooded during monsoon time. Extreme pleasure was breeded when we collected puff rice from our home and purchased excessive tasty Chanchur from the village shop to carry it to the bank and have fine time with many historical tales and facts. How can we forget all these things?

Many incidences regarding students have happened in my life which I will bear through out my life. I always tried to give top priority to my students and like me nearly all teachers do. I have taken many risk and challenges for them. I understand the socio economic condition of our Indian society. It is not always true that all students come from elite background but despite of their various obstrucles their parents have sent them to the elite schools. So the psychology and the problems vary from students to students. The best thing to observe a student is at the time of their tiffin. You can get a complete society inside the tiffin box. Whatever their financial status of their troubles engripped them, I have felt and seen, they have never been in misery to offer tiffin to a teacher. Two or three times I have been offered fruits, cakes and halua of carrot. I have eaten it with all hesitation but wouldn't return their request. Students can feel our weaknesses and we can feel their richness. The innocent bond in between a teacher and a student is as everlasting as our relationship to our family members and to god. It should never change. The capitalist venture has tried to rotten it up but it is so hot that it will never be frozen. The most beautiful relationship is once again built up after they leave the school and come to the school after years as a fresh university graduate in a distant state or come back to the school as an established professional. I have not included the student teacher relationship in the government schools. I am sure that the relationship in between a teacher and a student is as pure as crystal. This must be true to entire India and to the rest of the world. The psychology and the of innocence of the school students is globally same.

9

English Medium Schools without any Significant English Literary Growth in India

In 2001 I was reaching to Durgapur from my ancestral village which is hardly 15 kilometers away from Durgapur. I was surrendered to a situation which I have never faced as a rustic Bengali medium student who has learnt ABCD, I mean English alphabet while he was in class five. A group of girls students of Steel Carmel were speaking English so fluently. I was just trying to communicate to them in an embarrassing situation while they came down from the bus due to long queue nearby Kumar Mangalam Park, one of the biggest park in Durgapur. I could not talk to them smartly as I was from Bengali medium school. This was the bad effect of the then Jyoti Basu led left government whose slogan was "No English please, we are Marxist". This government has banned English in the Primary government school. But all people of Bengal were not Marxist. Why should we have to suffer for all government policies? We have learnt English in a very older age. But my incessant interest to learn English has laid my path viable, in consequence, within one year I started reading English newspaper without any hesitation.

I have been given the chance to read news in the school assembly. My fear was gone. So I did it regularly. I first wrote an English letter to my teacher who went to Cooch Bihar, his home town, during vacation. I can remember that I have shared this letter to my elder uncle who was an employee of Eastern Coal field Limited at Laudoha. He posted the letter to my teacher. My teacher was happy to receive it. However time and tide waits for none. I have come across many hurdles and struggled to learn English and still doing so as a conscious avid reader. After few years I have taught few students of Carmel school in my coaching class and in door to door tuition. One thing amazed me that even two students who failed in the previous class are sound enough to speak English. Were they to their best? They were actually weak in grammar and have no literary sense which many students lack in India.

Why the English medium schools are reluctant to promote literature? They are good in promoting science and sports and technology or spoken English. But they ignore the literary venture seems to be useless and non monetary. I have never seen in any School in personal experiences to edit an English magazine for their beloved students in a regular basis. The history of English language and literature is not taught. It is not there either in the cbse curriculum or in the icse curriculum. Two or three times I have seen wall magazines with below dignified content but it stopped for months. While I have tried to suggest the principal for its regularity they have shown no interest. I have been stopped to talk to the management regarding this issue. The good is not accepted, the useless things are cultivated at school. During my research I have visited to few schools for its enquiry but got no positive responses. I have talked to the students of different schools regarding whether they want a printed English magazine for literary growth, they were confused to reply but said there is no problems if they get. This is the initiative no one in school is willing to take. Neither it is costly affairs, not it difficult to continue but there is a negligence as it will give extra load to the teachers. But where is the significance of education without its literary growth? Science can breed happiness but literature may give creativity and inner peace which is mostly important in this disturbed world.Always we wanted our children to be a good doctor, engineer or high paid professional but we never wanted our children to a concious citizen who will think for the society at large. Literature acts as the mirror of the society. The cbse and icse board should make it compulsory for every school to edit at least a tri monthly literary magazine for balancing with the contemporanrity of English language like an English newspaper does. Every students should read the magazine once it is printed.It can serve the purpose of motivating the students also. The school itself may get a permanent exposure, back to the situation they always want to stay in limelight for their marketing agendas, by circulating it among the students. Generally every private schools in India love to call the newspaper or Television channels to promote their education even they did nothing good at all. So something to happen good in literary field is highly expected. Many schools may be publishing a magazines which I don't know. So many good residential schools may also have already done this. May not be also. After editing Indology Magazine for nearly eight volumes I have come to this conclusion that no one is ready to drive to buffaloes at jungle taking meals at home.

10

Psychology of the Parents in the Private Schools in India

We teachers of Bethany Mission School have been gheraoed on 2nd August 2021 at school campus by nearly hundred of guardians for the unexpected results of their wards in class xii cbse board exam. Indeed there was no exams this year due to Covid -19. This decision has been taken by Cbse board, it's headquarter is in Delhi and having various regional centers like Bhubaneswar, Patna, Allahad etc. There is no regional office in kolkata, the capital of Bengal and former capital of India during colonial period. There should have the regional office of cbse removed from Kolkata. However that 2nd august is a terrible day. I have never got such pressure in my teaching career like before. Marks were really unexpected. The students who were supposed to get 95 percent marks have only got 65-75 percentage of marks and those students deserve to get only 60 percent of marks got more than 85 percent. What a kingly joke it is to tolerate. We failed to satisfy the queries of the parents. In many ways Mr Saroj Sarkar tried to convince and console them but did go into vain. I was choked to explain while they were threatening us and shouting very badly like we were their paternal property or their slaves. We were locked inside the campus. The gateman was threatened to not to open the gate else to avoid any future course. They called the media and went to the NH 34 which was darely adjacent to Bethany Mission school. Policemen came and tried to convince them. We all were watching them from the campus. The policemen came inside the campus and talked to us. Saroj sarkar dealt so nicely with the police and the press. Rector J. Emmanuel was out of station for his cancer treatment in Delhi. In the same day the date for his chemo fell. I made a clever thing to control the situation. I just wanted to take a written complaint from the parents individually and collectively. Because I knew that the number now will decrease. After my declaration I found many of the parents who were shouting have kept their feet outside the school gate for they were afraid that we may preserve documentation for further uses. I got the benefit of my instant idea. I got only twelve parents put signature in a grievance letter. Results, I find, everything to the students and to the parents. Actually this is the reality of Indian Education System. In interview it works a lot. And many intellectual people have not got good government job and private jobs due to results. We were gheraoed that day from 9.30 am to nearly 7.30 pm because Delhi is too far from here. The Board is helpless to protect us. Covid was still going on. So we were not out of fear. As a result, many teachers were caught viral fever with extreme pain. Parents do not know that it for them we got the fever. This is one such instances. Many such incidences happened in the lives of the Private school teachers in India. Many ruckus have been created by the parents in the same day and after due to the same reason right from Techno India school of Balurghat to

Kalyani Public School Barasat and different parts of India. In ICSE board there were no such grievances came to public due to board results this year. There is a basic mistake the parents do they think that they have purchased the teachers as they are paying to the schools. This is very disgusting. This attitude should get changed. But on the other hand I have seen wonderful parents who love the school and the teachers in true concern. They leave everything to the hand of the teachers. Now I wish to share an interesting thing to you. Some eight years ago I have been questioned by Late Gulab Chand Sharma, the principal at Bal Mandir Senior Secondary School, Kishanganj, of why I have given more marks to a student rather than his performance. It was actually the query of the father of the students. I was confused to answer and I was just nodding my head. But the Guardian was too adamant. He was demanding real explanation. I checked my mistake from the answer sheet. He was supposed to get 28 but I have given 33 so that he could pass. I have applied my own license of teaching like a poet does while he composes a poem. Certain grammatical mistakes of poetry are not counted. In the case of William Shakespeare also, it happened. However I repeated that actually the student deserves to get only 28 but I have given him 33 so that he could pass. That guardian had opened his mouth by saying *"Jis bacchaghar pe itna battamij hota hai, woh pass keisa ho gaya"*. Always that boy fights with his father and kicks nose and *jina haram kor dete hai*. I started scolding the boy just like Hitler in front of Gulab Sir and his father. I just take a red pen and deducted five marks. I saw that his father got a relief and enjoyment. The student was crying bitterly. I came back to my residential room. But I did not know what the final decision principal has taken.

Thank god. I have never faced such situation for giving liberal marks to a student. I have not seen the boy in that school for a month. While I was in Durgapur I have never interracted with any parent of the school I taught. Only I used listen from the management and the lady principal that teachers must maintain the students diary very carefully and regulary as this is the only link in between students, Parents and Teachers. In Jammu I have got less chance to interact with the parents as I was there for few days. And in Kishanganj I have wonderful love and affection from the students whose father was a Border Security Force or SSB. Many times I have gone to their quarters with Gopal Singh, the music teacher at Bal Mandir Senior Secondary School. Gopal sir was having a limka book of record for playing synthesizer for a maximum period of time. We have been offered good food, tea or coffee and most interestingly we have given liberty to use the Canteen. Many item we used to purchase at lower price rather than the local market. We met many army officers there. They are really wonderful. I love them too. In Raiganj also I got the pleasure to go to kendriya Vidyalaya as a subject expert during their contractual teachers recruitment. Probably Commandant Sahab became the secretary of KV. So was the pleasure to meet during that time of selection. I have been invited three consecutive years along with many university professors and college assistant professors. Offering wonderful food and hot delicious coffee during interview was extremely energetic. The rest I love is the fortune to a sumptuous lunch with KV principal, Commandant Sahab and others. The neat and clean campus of Raiganj BSF always attract me to go there. A decade ago Gita Malhotra, a resource person of CBSE from Delhi came to train us in the same school. I should share few good and mixed memories of the guardians of SVM. There was a student's log book for each class teacher. And everybody used to be class teacher by the fault even one is not interested to take it. The system of collecting parents data was not bad indeed if a teacher is paid as per norms. But it doesn't happen in nearly 95 percent private schools in India. However all teachers were compelled to go the students whose class teacher was me. So nearly I had to go 40 houses. Maximum parents were Co operative and having good mentality in inviting us. But I had few bitter memories also. I have been obstructed ask the profession of the parents by few of them. But I had to do it fill the column. Nothing good will happen if I don't get this data. So I shall not force any parents. They have a right no to disclose it. Through parents teachers relationship drive many schools reveal the socio economic condition of the parents to get donations for the schools. Dr Banerjee, a military doctor, a retired and aged one, discovered by this hidden tricks. Later on I came to know that he had offered more than 15 lakhs for the growth of a hostel. His wife became my colleague who was a former principal at a school in Delhi. Everything was good but when the parents teachers meeting happened in school it was revealed that the parents behave just like a hungry tiger to a goat. This cinematic relationship is very hypothetical and it virtually last after the results of the board is over. Only intention was to get good number in practicals and others in the lower classes to the higher classes have become a general tendency from Arunachal Pradesh to Gujrat and From Kashmir to Kerala. But apart from all those things few parents were wonderful and exceptionally the relationship has last lasted till today like of few of the parents of my tuition classes. One of them is Rick and Olivia's father and mother. Kalpana kakima for whom I have a highest respect. Since the days I have taught them when little Rick and Olivia were at D.A.V Model School Durgapur. Few years ago Kalpana kakima lost her husband in cancer. It is nearly 14 years of relationship. Such many good hearted parents became just like my family members. Financial status of anybody has never become an obstruction. It is school which is indeed a temple of bond in between Students, Teachers, Parents and Management. Society will evolve to a noble hight if there remains a good balance in between the fours because schools always use to act as a miniature form of society. Last but not the least I wish to say that if you wish to see India in any part of India, do come to a CBSE or ICSE school, I am sure, you will be able to find this, positively.

11

Psychology of the Private School Teachers in India

Greek philosopher Aristotle wrote, "Man is a political animal," in his book *"The politics"*. At the same time he added that that true politics is never possible. Indeed politics is a universal subject and it is murkiest in India. No takes the responsibility to pull the mud from politics. On the other hand politics is the science of the government. Therefore school sectors should not indulge in dirty politics. There are three categories of teachers I have seen in my life. The first category of teachers they are busy in teaching only. Actually they are dedicated teachers. They don't bother politics surrounding them. But it happens always like a fly loves to sit upon stool. The second category of teachers are confused one. They can not move forward, they can not stoop. They can not shout for the development of the schools, they can not go against the management while any drastic action is taken. They are very meddling. But they have good appreciation. The first category of teachers are popular among students but neglected among the teaching fraternity. The third category of teachers in a private school are seemingly spies. They don't teach, they are hungry for luxuries and post. They are *khabrilal.* They give the information to the management softly and then they pass the information of the management to the teachers after filtration. In my twelve years of teaching career I have been separated in different occasions which gives birth uncanny wonder to of why I am not known the tiny things which the others know. While I have introspected I found the reason. And somehow I also belong to such category of teachers who love to survive without hammering others. I don't have any interest on what others are doing against me but I got an eye of experience to understand who the culprits are trying to push me to the hell.

Now a days I just fire the problems to concentrate upon studies.

We can not always blame the management as bad, teachers do often shows their raw paw among the fraternities. This extremely bad politics share a sheer district upon hope and situation. In government school politics is entertainment but in private schools a lot of depends on it right from job security to termination. The Hindi movies "Chalk and Duster" and "Pathshala " have rightly shown the internal politics of the teachers and the management.

Personal Experiences :

I will share some of the personal experiences which may meet to the fate of many private school teachers in India. Because Indians have same gene. The common link of Indianness may be found everywhere despite of our cultural or linguistic difference. After all we are run by a central system. So in executing the policies of the board the problems faced by different schools may be same. In discharging the duties of the board many teachers from different schools do gather time to time either in the exam center or in exhibition or in sports and other curriculums. Inter states programs do also happen. This is good for the health of education.As I am supposed to write my personal experiences regarding politics in school I should mention it that the female teachers in my first schools have done no polictics at all because I was the single male teacher in the teachers staff room. One madam suggest me, I can remind, to leave the school as I am a male teacher so I should not indulge much time to earn only small amount. She pointed out that many female teachers come to the school for time to pass. And they don't need money. In Durgapur many female teachers have wealthy husbands, it is not their essentiality to earn money out of private school teaching. The same explanation I have heard in other schools of different parts of India. Male teachers use to blame the female teachers for the entire salary pattern are so less because of the female teachers. Actually management people do prefer to recruit more female teachers for soft budget. Another facilities are found in recruiting female teachers are their less interest in keeping grievances or protest against the system. But this my explanation may not be always appropriate as I have seen many female teachers who chose the profession for their passion and for sustaining their families. I should mention Asha Arora madam of Bal Mandir Senior Secondary school whose husband was too old and her son was not established. Her entire family was lived on her single income. We live in a country where rice is finished before the salt is brought.

Politics is not bad if it cultivated with proper knowledge and vision. It may develop a good system. But what goes on in maximum Indian private schools is *"Chuglibaaji"*, I repeat it to be *Chuglibaji,* as I have heard this word from the teachers mouth. This is very interesting that one will speak to you so friendly in the beginning of the school, but he will turn to completely opposite before the parting of the day. There are many lobbies in a school. And one has to take part at least in a lobby for survival other wise one will be mentally disturbed without getting no support at all in his or her problems. This happened in a very confidential and professional way. When I was in a school in Raiganj I have tried to go against the system that one which stopped the voices of the teachers for decades. I wished to put voice to the voiceless.I thought that is I don't speak I would remain faulty. It was really praiseworthy that another madam P. Jain used to speak louder against the Vice principal who was a third graded man and a part of the management. She often called him a *chhagal* means goat in the open meeting. This was true that he was a *chhagal* who does have a brain without any intellectual ability of to hold a position like vice principal. But in India the man who holds power knows how to manipulate it and simultaneously if the management decides to give power to somebody will enjoy it till he is uprooted. This system of Power and dominion and manipulation have ended up India. This is the reason many highly intellectual people don't prefer to stay in India. They move to England or U.S.A. It is clear that the work culture and atmosphere is better there than India. At least *Chuglibaaji* must be missing there.

When you are a prey to politics you will get no favour. Your name will be striken out from many list. You photographs won't be printed in the soveneir, You won't be there in the school prospects. You won't be alloted leaves or every facilities other will get and you will see them getting more. These all things had happened to me because of the Vice Principal of the school in Kishanganj till I became a robust and vocal to directly complain to the secretary of the school. The principal was an empty envelope. However this Vice Principal was promoted to Principal after the death of the principal. The vice principal turned principal was an English teacher for whom many out stationed English teacher left the school being unable to cope up with his politics.This principal was having a team of *Chamchas,* a close group who took in conspiring others teachers who do not belong to their lobby. And interesting to add that this principle was terminated from the school due to some malpractices. So politics has his own answer.

12

Reactions from Different Individuals

Post Covid scenario has made drastic change in life of the private school Teachers and Lectures in Karnataka and in the rest of India. This book has been successful in exploring the facts. Mr. Binay Laha has rightly put the facts and figures and the struggle of the teachers who are mostly affected for decades specially in the post independent era. Actually private school teachers deserve a far better and dignified life than before as they are the builders of the Nation. Kudos to Binay Laha with whom I am long been associated in different debates and discussion regarding the holistic growth of school education in India, specially private school education and their teachers.

Vijay Mahantesh A Hosur

Academic Director and Head of operations Brilliant Public School and pre University College Bellary, Karnataka.

Although Modiji has accorded the stamp of Nation Builders on the Teachers' Fraternity, the covid 19 pandemic has exposed the real fact which nowhere shows any importance being given to the teaching community (specially towards private school teachers). There is neither job security nor monetary security. Every private teacher has to be a puppet in the hands of the Management. Those who dare to oppose the

Management are shown the exit gate. That's the fact. Mr. Binay Laha had been my collegue for three years where I noticed that he is a fighting soul. This work is possible only for a fighter like him.

Mithun Das,
PGT English,
St. Xavier's School,
Kishanganj, Bihar.

I have gone through the manuscript of this book. It is really awkward to read the odd things happened to the private school teachers through whom we have grown up as a ready human being. Personally I have read in icse and in cbse board. I am shocked to read the pathetic lives of the private school teachers in India. More shocking that the salary in a vernacular private schools start with only seven hundred and in many affiliated English medium schools pay their teachers more than lakhs. But exceptional does not prove the rule. The ninty five percent private school teachers must be paid as per norms. At least government should try to make a strict order of it. CBSE and ICSE both bye law write that a teacher has to be paid as per the salary of a government school teachers of the respective states. If the government schools teachers may enjoy all financial benefits including regular increment, simultaneously, private school teachers have the right to enjoy as because they are also given the status of Nation Builders. Praiseworthy Words and application should match together. All students those who have read through private schools must stand together with their beloved teachers. Thank you Binay Laha sir for raising the issues in favour of Private school teachers.

Sujata Saxena
Former ICSE and CBSE student,
Software Engineer
Mumbai, Maharashtra

India has a tradition of Guru Sisya parampara since ancient past. We have seen teacher like Chanakya who has been able to shape Chandragupta Marya as a wonderful king. In those times Education has a real value and the teachers have been respected just like a deity. But in present situation the respect of the teachers deteoriated. Management is one of the reason. They just do dirty business with private school teachers. They always think of how to remove a senior most teacher and recruit two teachers in place of him in almost little wages which is unfair. Some teachers do also take dirty policy of oiling up the management in blaming other teachers. But it doesn't invite any big profit. The education system has been in a total lapse in the last two decades. I have seen the worst scenario during Covid -19 when the teachers are changing their jobs and becoming a labour. Government is responsible for it.

I have been in the formation of a private school teachers group named PVT group in Gorakhpur, Uttar Pradesh. I have got many hundred teachers in the whatsapp group only but in reality I have seen teachers are fearful and selfish to come out to the street for a bigger protest. But always they talk of their deprivation in the staff room. They bother and should louder to the chamber of the management but while they need to talk in front of the management people, they become lollipop. I have faced many ideological clashes with management and teachers since decade. I can remember an incident when a teacher was slapped by a managent people, as in consequence, I tried to call all the teachers who sat idly on our whatsapp group and passed high sounding words but no body came to the street. I have seen a ray of hope when a group of private school teachers from West Bengal, holding a banner in protest of it, came to the streets and shouted for the causes of injustices happened to this teacher. But it was a great worry that the victimised teacher who wanted help from other teachers silenced himself .Teachers need to unite together to get justice and a better life. However I have written a poem for private teachers. Here it goes...

प्राइवेट शिक्षक

सितंबर 05, 2020

शिक्षक तो

शिक्षक ही होता है भाई।

क्यों और कैसा

अंतर पैदा करना चाहते हो!!!

क्या देखना चाहते हो,

उसके भीतर

कि वो प्राइवेट शिक्षक

सचमुच 'प्राइवेट' है!

जबकि सच तो ये है

कि उसकी कोई 'प्राइवेसी' नहीं है।

उसकी 'प्राइवेसी' पर लटकती है सदा

एक दोधारी तलवार !

जो बराबर उससे

घूर-घूर कर ये कहती है कि,

हर नया दिन

इस नौकरी का आखिरी दिन है।

शिक्षक को 'प्राइवेट'की गाली देने वालों

आसान नही होता ये सबकुछ.....

उसी दोधारी तलवार के धार पर

चलने जैसा है "प्राइवेट-शिक्षक होना"।

अपनी खुशियों को तज कर,

रखना पड़ता है,

स्कूल और बच्चों की

ख़ुशियों का खयाल।

'स्वयम्भू-देवताओं' की

तल्खियां सहकर भी

उनके आसवचनों पर

म्लान- मुख के

मरियल मुस्कान सहित

जबरिया 'थैंक-यू' बोलना पड़ता है।

और भी

न जाने कितना कुछ

न जाने किस रूप में

सहना पड़ता है।

हम भी पसीना ही बहाते हैं

और यथा सम्भव

आंख से रक्त का कतरा भी।

माना कि हम 'मज़दूर' हो चले हैं

और बहुत हद तक 'मजबूर' भी।

पर सनद रहे

हम चाणक्य की परंपरा से हैं

निर्माण और प्रलय

हमारी नियति के दास हैं।

Kunwar Rajyabardhan Singh
Senior most teacher
Gorakhpur, Uttar Pradesh

The book of Binay Laha "Private Schools in India and their Teachers" is all about the situation of the teachers and what they are facing in the private schools. Actually I have also observed in many of the CBSE schools that the teachers are not getting their salaries as per norms. On the other hand some teachers are forced to work at the minimum wages. Adding to the worry those schools are taking a high amount of fees from the guardian's but they are not providing proper salary to the teacher. In my personal life also I have seen many good teachers to leave the schools all of a sudden. This has hampered a lot to our study. In contemporary situation also the private school teachers are suffering a lot. During the pandemic of covid most of the teachers were not even salaried but the full fee were taken from the students. I have read through newspaper that few teachers left their jobs and became a street vendor or became a labourer during pandemic. Laws are there for private school teachers but in reality it is not implemented for their financial discipline and other facilities. This book tells about the situation of private teacher's from colonial rules to covid 19. Every former students and all other students having an inquisitive look upon the private schooling system in India may go through this book.

Deepak Kumar

Former CBSE student

Aspiring journalist.

BA- Journalism and mass communication

3rd year

The private schools in India and their teachers have rightly focussed on the suffering of the private school teachers in India. This book is a living history of the private school teachers in India. Kudos to Binay Laha

A. Chatterjee
Former Principal
Durgapur, W.B.

The book deals with the very common problems of the school education system of our time. The feeling and suffering of the private school teachers are nearly same in all parts of India. The teachers students relationship has been shown so nicely in this book.

Manish Chopra
Teacher at a CBSE school
Haryana

First of all I would like to wish my heartiest wishes to Binay Laha on writing this topic on the private schools and the suffering of their teachers.

I have been working in private school of cbse since last 12 years in different cbse schools in different parts of the Nation and always was cooperative with the school

Management as well as with the teaching fraternity but last year, specially, during pandemic pandemic I have faced many difficulties in terms of salary and security of jobs like many teachers. These too also have been painted realistically in this book.

There are many drawback in private schools such things I would like to mention here.

1. Most of the school are running in India in such a way that the appoinments letter are not given to the teachers. EPF and other leave facilities are not given.

Respect of teachers are detoriated day to day as everything is being exposed up.

Teachers are given unnecessary duty for documentation which does not have any direct connection to teaching.

Government is mostly indifferent to private schools. They are not ready to solve the problems of the private school teachers.

This book is a must read for Teachers, Management and for the students of the private school in India as it has nearly covered all contemporary issues including the history of private schooling from the ancient time ,though with a small reference, to Colonial intervention to Capitalist Venture.

Akash Tripathi

Senior Most CBSE Pgt Teacher from Uttar Pradesh.

A pain of private teacher can't be shared. Suddenly by reading this statement, a very simple question may arise in your mind 'Why not'. Why can't be shared? Is there any problem in it? Yes, of course, there are lots of problems. The main problem is that we are teacher, we are non government teachers. We create other professions, build the nation but can't save our position. It is the ultimate truth of the current situation. Many teachers have been thrown out from the well established and well developed school, forget about the averages." The current scenario is COVID19, where will we get the money?", the school talk.

Sell the property, sell one BMW car, you have enough to pay. Pay half, pay little,but pay. You can't hold it for six to seven months.

We are private teacher , can not share our pain. We teach the students how to unite the world , how to keep the patience in the difficult situation; but we don't have that much patience to follow the same lesson in our profession.

Mithun Chandra Ghosh

Teacher at a CBSE based school and a former student of CBSE.

From nursery till 12th, I have studied in private school. Today I am in a private engineering college in my 4th year and till now I have conducted several scientific research and won 4 national scale awards and recognitions. I believe it's all because of how I was groomed at school during my early years that had set a competitive mindset. The grooming was so perfect that I never required any private tutor at home. The school had taught me how to be disciplined, well mannered and be self-dependent in order to face life challenges ahead.

The relationship among the students and teachers were very friendly and supportive. I have never felt the difference between home and our school. They were supportive even outside of class and I have always been answered my queries during recess or even while travelling through our school bus. I have been guided from time to time on how to build my career. The relation among students across all classes was very friendly as well.

Infrastructure and lab facilities were always up to the mark. Classes were always held timely. At regular intervals, special sessions have been performed for enhancing communication and public speaking skills which include quizzes, debates and speeches during assembly. Special training had been provided for non-academics such as sports, music, dance, etc. One day per week was reserved for sports where we have received training on different athletics like long jumps, shot puts, etc. and other games like cricket, kabaddi, football, etc. Few classes were reserved for developing artistic skills as well where we were taught music and dance as per our choice. NCC and Scout training were also provided during different times where we were taught parades, etc. We have been taught gardening. Every year the school held an annual function where students performed and demonstrated their music, drama and dance skills. We had a picnic day every year where we had been often taken on excursion trips. Annual sports were conducted during December which had too many events on athletics and games. Special programs were also conducted during different occasions such as republic day, independence day, rabindra jayanti, etc. where special emphasis have been provided on nurturing the history and culture of our country.

Overall it was really amazing experience being a part of a private school and I would definitely recommend being a part of it.

Subhrangshu Adhikary

(Former CBSE student and presently an engineering student based in West Bengal.)

As a student of a private upper primary school, as I have read primary school at a government school, I can say that we have been much in care than the government schools. Private schools in west Bengal are always different than the government school. There is much care needed in the government schools in the present era. I have read Binay Laha's other books also. He always pen down in realistic ground. His book 'Act local think global' has focussed many contemporary issues. I am not as good in English so I have sent him my feed back in Bengali. He has translated it .As an employee of a central government I can understand the need of more security of the jobs of the private school teachers. They deserve to get better salary. I just thank my friend for always being active in writing for a greater cause.

Ashis Mondal

Former Private Bengali medium student and an employee in Eastern Coalfield Limited.

Sirsa, Paschim Bardhaman, West Bengal.

The greatness lies in this work is the exposure of truth. What have I learned from my teachers is that the truth itself is having a great strength. Our teachers at Srikrishnapur Junior High school ,a private school school, were extremely careful in our studies. After much struggle the school closed down for sociological and financial reasons. We have felt never such situations while we were students because we were to tiny tots to understand it. Now a days I feel the insecurity of a private sector job. I have been in a private sector for nearly ten years. And I feel same situation there also. But so far as education is concerned, the priority should be given to the private school teachers in all parts of our nation. We want to see a better tomorrow.

Achintya Laha

Former student at private school at Srikrishnapur and presently a private company employee.

Srikrishnapur, Laudoha Block, Paschim Bardhaman

This influential book will help readers in understanding the reality of the private school education in India. This is matchless. I found no body to pick up such topic what My friend Binay Laha has chosen. He has described so pathetically, if so happened in India, the shadow part of the glamorous private school.

Sudhakrishna Mandal,

Former student of a private school.
West Bengal.

I feel great to study in a private school. I am lucky because I study in private school because there are many students who don't get the opportunity to study in private schools. In fact I learned a lot from our teachers. I became intelligent by studying in private school that's why I feel proud of myself. I am happy. Although I get disappointed sometimes but I have no doubts about anything as the teachers clear all my doughts without any confusion. I have a dream that later on in the higher classes I will also study in other private english medium schools but for now Bethany Mission School is the best. I wish also to thank Kochi Kacha creche and play school at Birnagar as I have studied there and used stay in creche due to both my father and my mother are in teaching in different places. Thank you my father Binay Laha, who is a private school teacher and a writer for giving me the opportunity to write on this topic.

Aratrika Laha

Class three student at Bethany Mission school, Raiganj

There is an English proverb "Prevention is better than cure. The way the private school teachers are exploited must be stopped to get a better education system as nearly fifty percent of Indian students do read in private schools. Government should intervene to stop the exploitation of our gurus in Private schools in India. As a mother of a child who reads in private English medium school in Assam I always remain a well wishers for the teachers. We pay to the school not for encouraging dirty business of the owner of the school. We would be happy if the teachers are paid as per norms as the school can afford it.

Anjali Saikia

Mother of an ICSE based school student

Guwahati, Assam

I am a son of a Border Security Force. Therefore I have studied in different corners of India right from Pathankot to west Bengal to again in Jammu and Kashmir. I have wide variety of experience in mixing with friends and teachers in my country. I have seen teachers do face same problems in private sector. In KV the teachers are much stable and privilege. I have the pleasure to be taught by Binay Laha sir whom I miss a lot. Teachers are always guru. They should be given due respect despite of their financial status. Love teachers.

Krishan Kumar

Former Student of CBSE board

Samba, Jammu and Kashmir.

Poem

TEACHER - Our Future Maker

Giving us knowledge of something is a teacher,
Having an inbuilt experience feature.
A good teacher teaches us by heart,
And prays God for our peart.
A teacher helps us in developing our mind,
In such a way that is very kind.
A teacher teaches us tricks to achieve our goal,
And warns us to remain careful to avoid any thole.
Without the help of a teacher, we cant work rife,
And many difficulties will appear in our life.
In this vast world, they are teachers and parents only, on whom we can rely,
They always keep on us their eye.
And we are confident that they never tell a lie,
They gives us blessings so that we can fly high.
That's why, Parents are our caretaker,
And teachers are our future maker.

A former student of a CBSE school
– **Sahaj Sabharwal**
Jammu city,
Jammu and Kashmir, India.

I had admitted my son to DAV model school, Pandaveswar in the district of Paschim Bardhaman,

West Bengal. The school was very good. The teachers were too good. But I am from a rural area I could not continue my child to read in a private English medium school as good teachers were not available in our locality. So my son took admission in a government Bengali medium school. He can now read without much effort and good private tutors in Bengali medium are available. Mother tongue is sweeter than anything. I have just listened a lot of stories regarding English medium schools. These were not in favour of the teachers, not it was in favour of the students. But D.A.V. was good.

Jiban Laha

Father of Raja Laha and a businessman at Madhaiganj,
West Bengal.

I have been a student of private institute since I was small and had the privilege to be a student of the those for whom I am here Writting about them. The teachers of a private institute are not being remunerated for their contribution to the school.Instead of the fees we pay they are not so facilated.The infrastructure of the of the school are So well just to show and present but not for the use of students. The teachers are egar to give what they know to the students but the only problem is about the institute's permission.

A. Das

Former CBSE student and presently a medical student

Lucknow, Uttar Pradesh

Enough educational reforms were recommended by various committee. However the private school teachers have always been neglected due to improper implementation of the guidelines. There is an urgent need for a body which should protect the rights of private school teachers in India. The educational future of our country seem to be blink if these matter of concerns are not addressed on time.

Homnath Paudyal

Principal

Global Public Higher Secondary School

Surajpur Chhatisgarh.

I have read in a private School from class four to class eight. The rest of my life I have read in government institutions. I am now at the edge of forty. I can feel so deeply the care of the private school teachers.

Bibhas Laha

A former private school student and now a Panchayat Employee

Srikrishnapur, Pashim Bardhaman, West Bengal.

It has shown the evolution of the private schools from colonial intervention to capitalist venture. But the lives of the private school teachers in India remained non changing. The government should help the private school teachers in India for better growth of education as it has been observed that in many private schools teachers are exploited like anything. They are paid even less than the daily wage earners.

Saroj Sarkar

CBSE PGT teacher

West Bengal, India

Private school managements have a good tie-up with government officials and most of the teachers' complains are ignored or diffused or closed because of that.....Education now has become a lucrative business and that is the reason we have politicians, builders and all those who want to convert their Black money white in this arena. Wherever educationists are involved, they have created milestones, my respects to them....but time has come when government has to take very strict action against management of such schools who are flouting norms!!

Indranil Banerjee

Principal, Imperial Academy, Indore, Madhya Pradesh

I have faced nearly same situation in my career as a private English medium school teacher. Whatever is written in this book is an eye opener. I am hopeful that many private school teachers and management people in India will go through this book

Soumitra Mukherjee

CBSE based PGT teacher
West Bengal, India.

The overwhelming response to private schools in the last 2 decades is a signal of a big momentous shift in the mood of parents in educational sector in India. This should also be viewed as an acknowledgement of genuine efforts made both by school administration and its teachers, in particular in providing quality education to the children.

Now if we are truly desirous of transforming India into a powerhouse of education with institutions of excellence as we had in the past like: Nalanda and Vikramashila Universities, our private schools need to raise their standard a bit higher so that primarily, we can come to the par with global standard and then set up such institutions which become pioneer in this field.

Yes, the hardships of teachers are not hidden away from us. They haven't received what they truly deserve. Yet they have not shattered. They never showed their emotions, they never got agitated; a rare human quality only to be found in teachers. Here, I urge my fellow teachers to be a little more patient with themselves for darkness cannot hang on before our strong willpower and resolution. We will see better times for sure. Only we need to remain united to defeat the adversities we face.

Jai Hind

Nirmal Singh Arya

Teacher at Gyan Bharti Public School, Kotdwar

Uttarakhand

I am really thankful to all the parents, children and teachers of "Our Kochi Kacha Creche and play school .As a founder of the school I always remain happy when then children take education as a sport, enjoyingly. Similary I am thankful to the teachers of the school of my son and daughter in my town.

Ajanta Bakshi

Founder

Kochi Kacha Creche and play school

Raiganj, Uttar Dinajpur.

Accept my warm wishes for selecting such a crucial topic of the age. I wish all the success in your work. I am very happy that you were able to complete your dream book in spite of all the other demands on your time. You have done really a commendable job.

I am also heading a private school and can

understand the pain of teachers, their feelings and helplessness. How helpless a leader feel, when knowing that something is going unethical and illogical, still couldn't do anything to bring change. NGTO appeared to be a hope but it's failure took away all our hope and left many of us deserted and despair. I, my self was also associated with NGTO Rajasthan President and Media Spokes person with Binay Laha but now feel that it was worst decision and attending meetings - mere waste of time .

Emergence of Covid made it more pathetic. No rule is exercised in most of the private schools.

I must say Mr Binay Laha has portrayed the real suffering of private teachers in Covid era and illustrated it with fact & figure.

I hope to see more of your work in the future.

Dr Sunita Singh

Principal & Counsellor
Delhi Public School
President - All India Principal's Association, Rajasthan.

It gives me immense pleasure that my daughter is a student of a private English medium school in which I longed to become a student in my life. I have personally read in my nursery level at Rohini School which was a Bengali medium school. I am indebted to all the teachers in my life and thank those teachers who teach my daughter during the Covid -19 period regularly.

Tapashi C Laha

Teacher at a government school
Uttar Dinajpur, West Bengal

The condition of the teachers in Indian pvt schools is just like a chicken at the butcher's shop. The way chicken is not sure how long it's gonna live in the same way an Indian pvt school teacher is not sure that how long he or she will survive in a particular school/job . As the teachers grow old and his or her salary is supposed to get increaseat that time their hard time starts. *The future of the Future Maker (teacher) is in dark* _The question remains when teachers don't have a good future in the country then how can they make future of the kids?_ Unfortunately our political leaders are sleeping like a log turning a deaf ear towards the problems of pvt school teachers

Someone has rightly said that _"teaching is a work of heart, but what if the heart is only full of pain_".

But still I believe in the philosophy that, _influence of a good teacher can never be erased_.

Whole teaching community believe that one day there will be some transparency in our education system.

Neeraj Makwana,

H.O.D English
CBSE school,
Gujrat, India.

The book "Private schools in India and their teachers", by a remarkable author, Binay Laha, is probably the first book of this kind being published in West Bengal.

Private English medium schools are gaining more popularity across India. Eng medium school students are more prioritised and seem to gain more benefits than vernacular medium ones in case of higher education in colleges and in various other professional courses and workplace which made this the pre-eminent reason of glorifying English medium education!

Children of well educated and affluent families acquire more advantages than others. Lower and middle Class ones can't really adapt to the situation of paying higher amount of fees, buying new costumes frequently- for class, for games and for different annual functions every now and then !

It is often noticed that school authorities do not pay heed to the sayings and complaints of the patrons.

Corruption too has entered in the aspect of private tuitions,not just in English medium, but vernacular medium schools too play a role in disturbing students and pressurizing them to take tuition from the respective sub teachers for achieving higher grades in the respective practical based subjects.

Besides the number of corrupted and dishonest teachers, there are remarkable and honest ones too who vow to teach better and bring out the best in their students yet do not achieve that deserved respect many a times!

There is also a prevailing misconcept that budding teen students get spoilt in an English medium school.

Just as not every single stuff is bad around us, similarly all private English medium schools doesn't justify the aforementioned critics. There are premium English medium institutions across the nation that continue to their records of shaping successful students and hence notable alumni and dutiful, well educated, and most importantly "a better Human Being in progress" have been from such english medium schools.

Ava Sarkar Mandal

(Writer and the mother of two ICSE students)
Raiganj, Uttar Dinajpur, West Bengal

13

Interview

This is an interview taken by Pankaj Bhalla. He has served as a senior most PGT and still teaching in the state of Haryana and performed many administrative posts. He always believes in the reformation of the private school education system in India. Goes the interview.

Pankaj Bhalla: Namaskar Binay, Good afternoon sir

Binay: Good afternoon sir and Namaskar to you.

Pankaj: How is your health now

Binay: Now I am improving gradually. I thought that there were only four stitches, but while the cover was unveiled I found it is six. Actually I have not got much pain during the operation but before anesthesia I got excessive pain in my my right hand where the lump was there. It was actually adjacent to the place where we take vaccines. However the antibiotics are still being taken and stitches are still not removed. Tomorrow I will move to the doctor for doing it.

Pankaj: Well. That is a good news. But what about your reading and writing?

Binay: See Pankaj sir I am an avid reader since my childhood. But till class ten I have focussed most on textbook. I can remind that I used to read text book more than ten times to ruminate and to score good marks, indeed to become first in the class. And I stood first for long six to seven consecutive years in my school life. I have forgotten only what I have been in class two. Directly I have been promoted to class three in the mid of the session, so far as my knowledge is concerned. But you know it hampered a lot in my class ten examination. I was too tiny then to understand difficult mathematics. I have given my class ten when I was hardly forteen years old. And about my writing I am always enjoying right from composing poems to article writing and working on my present book *"Private Schools in India and Their Teachers"* which I have been writing for long period of time during lock down. Actually lock down has locked many scope but simultaneously it has opened many possibilities of reading and writing. I have purchased nearly 30 thousands rupees of book which I consider to be a bulk amount for a teacher like me. But as an avid reader I can't resist myself in reading. And I just give order to those authors whose ideas are matched with me. Oh ho I have forgotten to mention that one more book is going to be published in Bengali. This is a collection of short stories named Tumuni. I have got a small note from Uday Shankar Durjay, my friend and a writer from England. He runs an English magazine that is Pol. On the other hand I edit *Indology* Magazine.Vol IX of *Indology* is going to come up soon.

Pankaj : Good to hear from you. But one thing is not clear to me. You stay in Raiganj, the Sadar town of Uttar Dinajpur District you told me. But you are not originally from this place. Can you please share your journey to your beloved readers and to me also. Indeed I took interest in reading your works. I have heard you organize Indology Literary meet at WDCOC, Raiganj.

Binay : Yes Pankaj sir for you specifically, and for all in general, I wish to share my journey from Durgapur to Raiganj. Indeed I grew up in a village named Srikrishnapur in the Durgapur Sub division of Undivided Bardhaman district of West Bengal. Later on it became a part of Paschim Bardhaman. I took my early education at Srikrishnapur Primary School. Later on I read in Junior High school at Srikrishnapur. This school was a private school managed by group of educators and few local people. This school school was wonderful in promoting education and competition. I learnt English alphabet in this school while I was in class five. But one teacher whose techniques of teaching helped me to catch this language with interest. He is Subhas Sarkar Sir. Basically he was from Gosamari of Kuch Bihar district of the Northern part of West Bengal. I mean the area where we are living now. Though Kuch Bihar is too far away from Our Raiganj City. After completing my class ten from Gourbazar Rampada Uchha Vidyalaya I went Durgapur, the city of literature I write. There I passed class twelve with a very good marks in arts stream. Later on I choose Raniganj TDB college for my graduation though I have got chance in Durgapur Government College. I could have taken admission in all colleges under the University of Burdwan, popularly known as Bardhaman University, wherever I choose to go for my expectedly good results. Later on I have been in kolkata for a long period of time of no less than five years. Then again I returned back to Durgapur for financial problems at home. I started tuitions for earning money in a very professional way. But before it have been a tutor during my graduation also. However after completing my post graduation I got selected at a private school in Durgapur. The salary was too meagre.

So out of disappointment I left it for bigger gaining. In the meantime I married. Then I have had to shift to Kaliyaganj, a small town hardly 25 kilometers away from Raiganj. I joined at Bethany at Hemtabad. Later on I got selected at SVM Raiganj. After teaching there over years I shifted to BMSS kishanganj in Bihar. Then I came back to Raiganj few years back. And presently I am teaching at BMS, Raiganj, Which is the oldest English medium school of the entire Uttar Dinajpur District.

Pankaj: Thank you for sharing all in details. Now I wish to know from where you got the interest to write down your book *"Private School Teachers in India and their Teachers"*.

Binay: It is true that I am a writer since 2000. I have the pleasure to see the end of twentieth century and the beginning of twenty first century. The situation always had helped me to become a writer. Now presently we are running through a very difficult time of our lives. We have seen more than forty lakhs people to die during lock down period due to Corona pandemic. It has devastated the lives of the private school teachers in India and obviously the workers in private sectors at large. We don't know how many people lost their jobs or remained starved. The socio-economic suffering of the private school teachers have pushed me to think in this way because I do personally belong to this field.No school No fees movement has shown the exact face of this system. This is the grave reason to feel for my fraternity. But covid is not the only factors to feel for our teachers or for their teachers. I remained mostly sensitive from my early childhood when I have seen my own teachers to loose their jobs as this school was a private one. Later on in twelve years of teaching have fetched me many realities. I have seen many of my colleagues to get terminated from school even at the time of their dark phase of life like the death of somebody's father. I can remember that one of my friend lost his father and in the same month he lost his job. I have seen closer the volatile decision of the school management upon teachers. I have seen 18 teachers to get verbal termination from school I taught. What is this education all about? When a guru is terminated, it is a crime I consider. I have seen a lady teacher was crying after her seventeen years of service at a school and when she was forced to resign no one, even the principal, asked her the cause. I too became the pray of it as I was raising questions as I found that the education was collapsing. How can we tolerate being a teacher to see education falling to darkness under some idiotic decision of the management. I have seen the gutkhakhor secretary was advising the teachers to not to sit in the tea shop and to smoke as teachers are their personal properties. It was strange to watch the illiterate activities of the management to run an English medium school. It is a matter of shame and fun when I see the management people don't even know how to write or talk in English but they are misusing their money and muscle power by utilizing the government machineries. I wonder why the government education officers remain so indifferent to this situation years after years. And above all I find the lack of order, philosophy, vision and spirituality of the management to run the institutions. The picture is same everywhere in India. You can go anywhere and get the same tragedy except five percent schools. I have divided the Indian private schools in two categories. In one category five percent schools belong. They maintain norms as per government. Sometimes better than this. The rest ninty five percent of private schools do not follow any norms. And they are just playing with education system. There is a need of vast change for better growth of our country. Apart from this situation I have been associated to the similar field of research for few years. During lock down period some discussions with Dr A. Das and Dr M.K. Hasan regarding my PhD topic and synopsis helped me to shape up my ideas after reading books on this similar juncture. Prof Rup Kumar Barman has motivated me for my general writing on contemporary topics in the newspaper. I have gone through his books have enormously helped me to understand the contemporary research techniques. I was in initial discussion with my publisher whose motivation has put extra mileage to my book. I have learnt some technical things from him to complete this book.

Pankaj : Why do you emphasize much on the salary of the private School teachers?

Binay : This is their right. They must be given as per norms. Otherwise government should change the bye laws for private school and should write that salary is the subject of the particular school. They may give 700 rupees per month to a teacher which I have elaborated in one chapter that there is big gaps in between salaries. It varies from seven hundred to two lakhs. I doubt whether the average income of the private school teachers in an affiliated school is Ten thousand rupees per month. It is clearly written in the bye laws that a cbse or an icse teacher shall be paid as per the standard of a government school teacher. Is it happening in India? Tell me who is responsible? I or You or others? Is there less pressure of jobs of a private school teacher? I don't think so.

Pankaj : Don't you find that there is a need of organisation?

Binay: Absolutely. Otherwise teachers will be terminated as flies to wanton boys. Shakespeare might be true in this regard. Taking this vow we have started a movement under the banner of CITO means CBSE and ICSE teachers organisation. We have gone to the streets and shouted louder for many reasons, successively. We did have our five demand. Security of jobs, salary as per norms, introduction of EPF to every teachers, leaves and others perks and transparency of the system we included. Initially we failed but it was having a bigger impact. We merge it to PVT organisation of Uttar Pradesh. Later on to another organization for our stronger goal. We have got the benefit to connect private school teachers through out India. Now we can share our problems to each other. Now an Organization called NIPTA is doing wonderful job. Many organizations will come up and they will solve the problems gradually. But though CITO failed initially, but I believe, it has shown the guts to face the media and to go for street demonstration for the first time in West Bengal and in India.

Pankaj : Don't you think that teachers need to take legal support?

Binay : We are living in the largest democracy of the world. So we should move to the court if we face severe problems. Court is the better way for reformation. I have gone to lawyers few times and been able to solve few problems. Few yet to be solved. But open discussion is another way left to us also. Generally we should not prefer the first to exhaust our money and energy like a patient to a private chamber of a doctor.

Pankaj : Don't you think teachers too are responsible for diminishing the system?

Binay : Yes, In one of the chapter I have elaborated about the psychology of the teachers. Teachers too are engaged in doing mud slinging to each other which must be stopped. Worry to add that in Indian society politics has become an integral part of any administration. Survival politics is not bad but harmful polics is not a welcoming note in the educational institutions. Education is after all an education. Whether this is to be imparted in a corporate institutions or to a rural institutions. The basic pattern of education will never change. The simple thing is that we have a syllabus before us, we have to teach the students and we have to make our students a good citizen. That is all. I don't not understand why is there so much of chaos and doldrums. Teachers personal gaining should not be connected to the obstruction of education. Tuition manipulation happens oftentimes. It should be stopped. Above all one should remain correct to oneself. That is all.

Pankaj : Any recommendations?

Binay : I have elaborated it in one chapter.

Pankaj : How would you define the ancient and medieval system of private schooling system?

Binay : Yes, that is a nice question. In every thing I find a historical link to the present system of education. Like in ancient times education means *"Asodoma Sadgamaya, tomoso ma jotirgamaya, mrityorma amritanggamaya* means to lead me rom falsehood to truth, lead me from darkness to light, lead me from death to immortality. This has been nicely described by Jagdish Chand in his book *Education in Ancient and Medieval India*. Teachers were highly respected and they were treated as Guru Brahma .Even we have seen that in medieval India there were several village schools where the teachers used to get remuneration out of kind, though not in cash. The colonial period was not bad but teaching in private English schools were reserved to the Europeans but later on the situation changed. The last 70 years have been worst for private school teaching job. And Covid 19 has shown the nudity of this system when teachers are leaving their jobs for they are not paid.

Pankaj : In your view how do the private school management exploit the private teachers ?

Binay : 'Modus of operendi' adopted by large number of schools to exploit the private teachers is as follow:

1. They do not show the service rule book of school to teachers
2. They don't fill the post of teacher in Contract of service, Teacher didn't know whether he is appointed against a regular post or leave vacancy. Later on they will fill it as suitable to them.
3. They didn't give them the appointment letter containing all the terms and conditions
4. They didn't give confirmation letter to teacher even after completing the probation period.
5. They illegally deduct one month salary as security money in certain schools.
6. They didn't give all the leave benefits to teachers
7. They didn't follow the procedure (given in CBSE affiliation Bye laws) of disciplinary action against the teacher.

They directly terminate the teachers.

8. Some of the schools deposit the salary in bank account of teachers and large part of salary amount is returned back by the teacher to school.
9. They didn't maintain the service book of the teachers.

So in my view all the teachers should go through the chapter 5 of CBSE affiliation bye laws to know his or her rights.

Pankaj : Well, What is your view on online classes? Is it healthy?

Binay : There is no substitute of online classes now in its present scenario during pandemic. And at the same time it is not the substitute of the traditional classes. The poor classes of students have in pressure to purchase smart phone or laptop. The teachers too have suffered. Many teachers who do have the capacity to purchase a laptop they have taken loan to purchase it. But because of this flow of education people still are preferring to send their children to a private school. Obviously they are afraid to send their children to a government school except few exceptions had happened in Delhi though the ground realities are not known. Due to online classes many teachers who are not capable to adjust with technology have lost their jobs. In Madhyapradesh on line classes were off, as in turn, parents did not pay, so the teachers were not paid. But it has created many virtual job of teaching. Those who can excel have turned the problems into possibilities. Online classes are helping to become education more privatised. Many problems erupted out this year due to no examination system. Giving marks on a priority basis or prone to possibility basis have failed to give quality education.

Pankaj : You have worked on a pan Indian topic. Don't you find a gap in between.

Binay : May be. But the problems through out India are same from colonial intervention to capitalist venture. The 1992 liberalisation of PV Narsima Rao government has rottened up the system. Only earning money should not be the outcome of education. Government should take care all kinds of teachers in India whether government, semi government or private school teachers. But obviously government should take care of the private school teachers as a must priority, as it is my observation that every private school teachers think four times about the management in every ten minutes while there are in the school. This hegemony should get a change.

Pankaj : What is your view on other teachers in the private institutions in India like private college or private university professors?

Binay : This research to be done by them only. I don't know their problems exactly. But it might remain same.

I have been associated with some private self financed college and universities.I came to know that they are not happy too. It is a loss for entire Nation while the teachers are not happy. See, nearly all professional including doctors, engineers, Pilots etc are taught in a secondary or in a senior school. If you see the data of the success rate I am confirmed that most of those are from private English medium schools in India.

Pankaj : Any other projects you are dealing with?

Binay : Not now. I am busy in reading few more books and I am writing few articles on other topics.

Pankaj : Thank you very much for bearing with with me and helping me and your readers to understand the entire journey.

Binay : Many many thanks to you Pankaj sir for guiding me in the right way by throwing various queries and questions. Actually I have enjoyed a lot. Thank you all my readers. Thank you.

(The interview was taken on 15 September 2021 virtually. It was drafted accordingly).

14

Recommendations

"Paritranaya sadhunam
Vinasaya cha duskritam
Dharmasansthapanarthaya sambhabani juge juge."
Chapter 4, verse 8

Bhagavat Gita

In his book "The Argumentative Indian" Noble laureate Amartya wrote, "The salary of teachers in regular schools has gone up dramatically over recent years, even in real terms, that is after correcting for price changes. This is an obvious cause for celebration at one level (indeed I remember being personally involved, as a student at Presidency college fifty years ago, in agitations to raise the desperately low prevailing salaries of school teachers. But the situation is now very different." This is indeed a fact that the teachers in the government sector are happy in India in terms of their salaries. Revolution happened from many apartment. So they have got the benefit at last. The most wonderful things of the government school teachers that attract me is their unity in terms of their rights and opportunities. They always take legal help.

So if the government school teachers united go to the court for their rights and justice, why not the private school teachers? Law is equal to everyone in India. Worry to add the private school teachers have failed to make kolorab means shouting louder for their rights. Very few teachers in this sector have sacrificed for the benefit of others.India is a country of resistance. Our writers have shown their guts to speak the truth and sacrifice. Nobel laureate poet Rabindranath Tagore rejected Knighthood, which was given by the British, as in protest for the deadly Jaliwanbag Massacre. Subhas Chandra Bose did not continue his ICS job which was the mostly prestigious job to liberate India from the bondage of the British rule. Laxmi Bai of Jhansi sacrificed for the cause of the nation. Our Father of the Nation Mahatma Gandhi did live a luxurious form of life even he was a barrister. They have always shown the way to us. But the private school teachers failed to create a resistance against the corrupt government officials who do not act as per the instructions of the government. If they would have acted problems could become lesser. I have given the cbse and the icse bye laws of 2016 which are the enough evidence of why teachers need raise voices for their justice, if they think so. Many years ago I shocked to listen from a teacher who told that the management do have their right to terminate a teacher as it is just like a maid and master relationship. He was indeed in favour of the management that time. After few months he has been terminated and he came to me and told this is totally injustice to terminate a teacher. This dual and selfish minded people are spoiling up the unity of the teachers. Every teacher who will join a school as a fresher must claim the appointment letter as this is their constitutional rights. But teachers do not ask it as they want their job first. And they become satisfied but later on they won't get any chance to produce it for their legal document. Teachers do not demand salary as per norms, they just want their entry gate .This becomes easy for them to get a job on a verbal commitment, similarly, they are shown the exit gate in more easiest way. It depends on you whether you want good amount of salary.Teachers,in maximum schools, do not enjoy EPF and other facilities which must be done compulsory by the government other wise government should deaffiliate the instructions. But who will bell the cat? Every teacher shall be given the experience certificate ,on demand, leaves should be given, as per norms and maternity leaves should be given to the female and paternity leaves should be given male teachers. Many female teachers are obstructed to join after their maternity leaves which is a deadly crime. I believe that one has to be a fearless. One interesting thing I wish to share now. While I was collecting the responses and reactions from different individuals I got a positive vibes from a Delhi based teacher who ignores the next day to print his name. He was just sharing that he will leave the school and choose the profession as a lawyer as he had obtained his L.LB too but he will not work under any pressure in the school. I and my friend from Uttar Pradesh Kunwar Rajyabardhan singh have tackled too cases so nicely, without loosing our temper or making any rough behavior, we have stopped two termination and we have been able to force a management to give sixty thousand rupees to a teacher who was terminated due to no good reason. We have seen very closely few employees at DEO have promised us to solve the problems of a lady teacher but on it came to our observation that even the DEO patched up with the concerned school management and delayed the case so that the victimised teacher left her energy to fight. It is difficult to keep up patience for a long time to get justice. On the other hand many teachers, after taking the help from other teachers, forget them and once they indulge in same bitterness. Some after getting a solve disconnect with the teachers group as they thought groups as a political organization. This is common mal practice of the management that while a teacher will raise questions ,he will be blamed to be political and he will be separated by everyone but doing politics is a constitutional right. No can blame upon it. The owner of the schools are doing every politics and they take the help from the politicians. They invite politicians to show their power. They want protection too. We understand it. Other mal practices are managent do collect few grievances from the parents by manipulating them and threatened the teachers for his inability to teach even he is teaching for 25 years. These all are valueless. I have faced few such incidents in which I was asked why I have taught references and not completed the syllabus by a vice principal. At once I wanted to know the syllabus from his mouth. He told it was syntax that I have not taught them. I answered the vice principal that "Your very Syntax 'is not in the syllabus. He just stopped. One more time I have faced an award things when I have been blamed that I tutored some students being a residential teacher. I asked him whom I teach, please tell me the name. He failed to answer. Private schools in India are running in such a way where no body is ready to listen to your problems. If you are frustrated, you have to face the destiny. Teacher need to get united being an Indian and as a conscious citizen. It is through incessant struggle the labours in England, got their rights, to reduce the span of time to their daily works from a forced period of time to eight hours after Industrial revolution in England. The Entire world has got the benefit. Now no company or factory can force a labour to work more than eight hours a day. This is protected internationally. I have had the pleasure to talk to two lawyers of the Supreme Court of India. One is from Tamil Nadu and another is from Delhi. Both have the same version of suggestions. They used to say me that court is the only ray of hope for the private school teachers as as for bringing justice in our Nation. I have talked to a lawyer, in Bolpur, who told me that it is a criminal act to work without appointment letter. To not to offer appointment letter to an employee is also criminal. I met few more lawyers in Kolkata and in Benares. One has become my friend for closest proximity of our names. I met him at Beneras ghat. He suggested us to solve problems either by consultation or teachers should unite together. One of my college friend who became a lawyer later on loves to listen if we are choosing the way of law. Similarly I just wish to add that teacher may individually reform the system through his individual struggle which I have long practised for the benefits of others. On the other hand these all aforementioned mal practices must be stopped for transparency in the education system.The same system that has been practised from the colonial intervention to the capitalist venture has had to get an end.Every progress comes through an evolution. Even, we human beings, have got our beautiful body and mind after incessant struggle with nature and ourselves in internally and externally. We can not ignore the Darwinian struggle for existence and survival of the fittest. Many strange things have happened on earth. Many vast changes occurred in the education field. No one has ever thought that the Delhi government education system will become a role model for the rest of India. The education minister of Delhi Shri Manish Sisodia has tirelessly tried their level best with their teamwork which I came to from Shiksha, the book is itself a motivation for shaping up a vision. Their team should keep an eye for equality for the better ment of all the private school teachers in Delhi so that it can be a role model for the nation. I will appeal all kind hearted politicians, MLAS and MP s and ministers, specially the education minister of all states and Central education minister to be with the private school teachers in our beloved India. This thing will become very easy if they instruct the concerned department. I will appeal all private school teachers to write to them regularly so that they may not forget our words. It is our moral duty to knock to the district education officer to remind them their duty to protect us as one of the teacher from Rajasthan wrote to me that private school teachers are just like a chicken to the hand of butcher as they do not know when will they be sacked from the school like that of the chicken. This is really pathetic when a teacher feels such. A teacher with the fear of his own job can never be able to teach to his best. This is a partial collapse of education. A picture, in the social media,has remained viral for years while we see an old lady teacher of a private school became a begger, at the same time, her old photo with bright students are pasted. We don't want to see our future in this way. I, at the same time, expect that our honorable Prime Minister will organise a nation wide campaign to give respect to the private school teachers in India each year. Indian private school teachers should connect private school teachers of other nation to interchange ideas, education process and traits, method and application. If possible, international forums should also be formed because except few countries, maximum countries do bother less about the private school teachers. Finland, England, America may be to their best. But what about others? Teachers should stand together, in the words of Swami Vivekananda, to arise, awake and stop not till the goal is reached About the author. Time and again I just wish to say that we are born for doing something better in this world. Last but not the least I will be happy if all private school teachers support those teachers who are trying to lead in a local or district wise of for the nation for the welfare of us and you. We ought to support them. At the same time we all are thinking for the growth and development of India through best quality of Education. For our security we may invite the fourth pillars of our Democracy. The printing and electronic media and social media may help in building confidence. Teachers may also take their pen to write in the newspaper in the open forum which I am doing for a long period of time. Many may laugh but many thousands will be protected as it is exposed up to the lakhs of people. We have to think our nation despite of many troubles. Very recently I was going through" The shape of things to come "of our former judge of Supreme Court, Markanday Katju has opined many good things to promote indianness. In his essay What destroys a Republic? What Unites it? I have gone through few wonderful lines of Subhramania Bharathi who wrote this poem in Tamil in 1910. This is a good instance of Indianness. It reads -

"Mupadhhu Kodi magamudayal
Enil manipuram ondrudayal
Ival sepumozhi padhiinetudayal
Enil sindhanai ondrudayal "

"This Bharat Mata has thirty crores faces
But her body is one

She speaks eighteen languages

But her thought is one ".

So at the same time we the private school teachers may cultivate indianess through our organization of thought in teaching our students the about our multi cultural and multi lingual nation. We have to dream for a better world and have to come out from all pessimism. All private teachers in India must unite together with a promise to walk together before our ending scene of the theatre of our lives.

And I always remember Lord Tennyson in any good things to do ...

"Death closes all

But something ere the end some work of noble note may yet be done "

Binay Laha

Pgt History

Bethany Mission school

Raiganj, West Bengal.

Newspaper Clippings

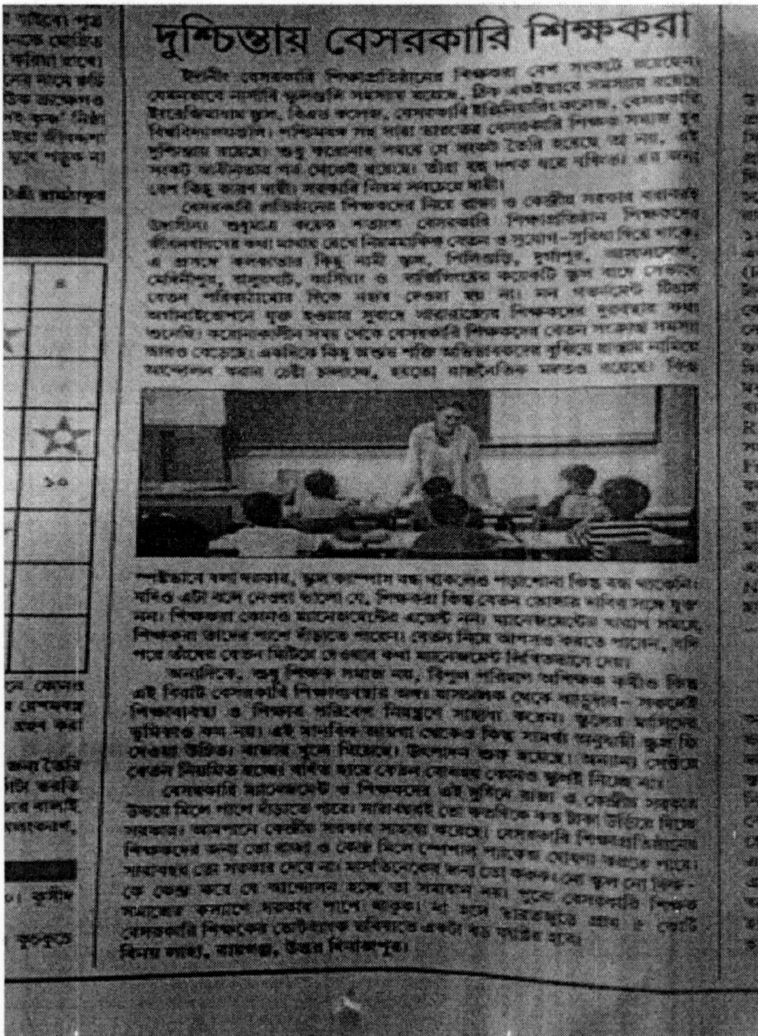

দুশ্চিন্তায় বেসরকারি শিক্ষকরা

Reg. No. 03/27/01/22476/20

Non Government Teachers Organization (NGTO)

Email: ngto.in@gmail.com, Website: www.ngto.in
Office: 403, Pukhraj Coorporate, Navlakha, Indore, Madhya Pradesh

Pankaj Bhalla 8307819616 National President	Alok Nagar 9826278783 National Secretary	V. K. Nagar 9424419924 National Coordinator

Ref. No./ PMO/NGTO/sugg/01/2020 Date: 04/07/2020

To

Shri Narendra Modi

The Prime Minister of India

Sub: Deemand By NGTO for Upliftment of Private Educaters.

NGTO, the "national" organization of employees of the private education sector, demanded from the Central Governments to conduct an unbiased investigation into the irregularities in private educational institutions and to provide relief packages to teachers and other employees for the emergency arising out of Covid-19.

The "National" Non Government Teachers Organization has been receiving frequent complaints of non-payment of salaries and expulsion of employees working in various parts of the country due to the closure of private educational institutions in emergency arising out of Covid-19. With this, crores of teachers across the country are facing a severe economic crisis, and are being forced to sell vegetables or to work as laborers.

The news of teachers committing suicide from all over the country is also a matter of concern.

Do governments and political parties only see the vote bank?

Since teacher suicide is not a political issue and no political party is going to benefit from it nor are there any elections yet to be held, the employees of the private education sector have been left on their own. This is a gross injustice.

Both the present and the future of private teachers who make the future of the children of the country are in danger. If this situation remains, then the day is not far when private educational institutions will find it difficult to find teachers and employees.

Another very important thing here is that all the private educational institutions in the country are all NPOs or VOs i.e. Non Profit organization or volunteery organization. So it is clear that the management does not have any right over the income from these, and no trustee or member can hold any profit post. So how did the management who did not even have a bajaj scooter, roaming in Mercedes today it is a matter of investigation, where did the property of crores, bank balance, expensive vehicles come from?

Also, when talking about the process of recognition, corruption has spread from head to toe, if a fair investigation is done, the recognition of more than 90 percent of the institutions can be canceled.

Why validation applications are not canceled? How is any institution recognized?

The Teacher is Never Ordinary,
Holocaust and Creation Flourish in His Lap!

Reg. No. 03/27/01/22476/20

Non Government Teachers Organization (NGTO)
Bihar
(A National Organization For Private Educators)

Website: www.ngto.in, Email: ngto.in@gmail.com, Contact No. 9424419924
Head office: 403, Pukhraj Carporate Navlakhha Indore 452001

Ref. No. : 01 Date: 26th May, 2020

The District Education officer,
Kishanganj,
Bihar-855107

Subject : Received a complaint letter
Respected Sir,
We have received a letter from a post graduate teacher Miss [illegible] Singh of Orienta[illegible]hool, Kishanganj against the non-payment of the salary. She has also added about the conditional payment, i.e., salary would be paid only after the resignation from the job.
Therefore we request you to look into this matter seriously. For this act, we'll be highly obliged to you.

With Regards,
Mithun Chandra Ghosh
State President of Bihar, NGTO

Binay Laha
State President of West Bengal and In-charge of East Zone
(Bihar, Jharkhand, Orissa, West Bengal), NGTO
Mobile: 9564926834

The teacher is never ordinary,
holocaust and creation flourish in his lap!

The Teacher is Never Ordinary,
Holocaust and Creation Flourish in His Lap!

Reg. No. 03/27/01/22476/20

Non Government Teachers Organization (NGTO)

Email: ngto.in@gmail.com, Website: www.ngto.in
Office: 403, Pukhraj Coorporate, Navlakha, Indore, Madhya Pradesh

Pankaj Bhalla	Alok Nagar	V. K. Nagar
8307819616	9826278783	9424419924
National President	National Secretary	National Coordinator

Due to the involvement of the management and the District Education Officer, the service rules of the school staff are being stripped, if any teacher dares to approach the District Education Officer to complain, he is removed from the job, that is why the other teacher And employees are not able to complain against the management.

Staff service rules prescribed by Education Boards / UGC / NCTE and other related departments are not being followed by the educational institutions.

According to FICCI, 43% of the total students of the country study in private educational institutions.

The government is also earning a regular income of billions of rupees every year from the fees of registration, recognition, renewal and various types of examinations of private school / college / and university institutions.

As an example, just look at the income of board exams in Uttar Pradesh, if we only talk about the fees charged from students appearing in 10th / 12th, then Uttar Pradesh alone has 30,24632 in 10th and 12th in the last year alone. 25,86440 A total of 56,11,072 fifty six lakh eleven thousand seventy two students were involved, whose examination fee is Rs 500, Rs 600 from regular students and Rs 700, Rs 800 from self-help students respectively, thus only through board examinations from Uttar Pradesh alone to the government Income of Rs. 364.7 crores.

It is estimated that in the whole of India, only 10 and 12 exams (regular / self-study / and open) were conducted in which the government earned about 20,000-30,000 to twenty thousand to thirty thousand crore rupees.

Therefore, it is the responsibility of the government to provide financial relief to the employees working in private educational institutions in this odd situation, and to take strict action to follow the Employee Service Rules prescribed by the Boards of Education / UGC / NCTE and other related departments.

Therefore, the NGTO demands from the central and state governments that

A separate grievance redressal department should be set up for employees of the private education sector.

Strict adherence to the employee service rules prescribed by the Education Boards / UGC / NCTE and other related departments.

There should be a fair check at the ground level of registration documents, recognition documents and salary and other facilities available to employees of private educational institutions.

Pankaj Bhalla
National President
NGTO

The Teacher is Never Ordinary,
Holocaust and Creation Flourish in His Lap!

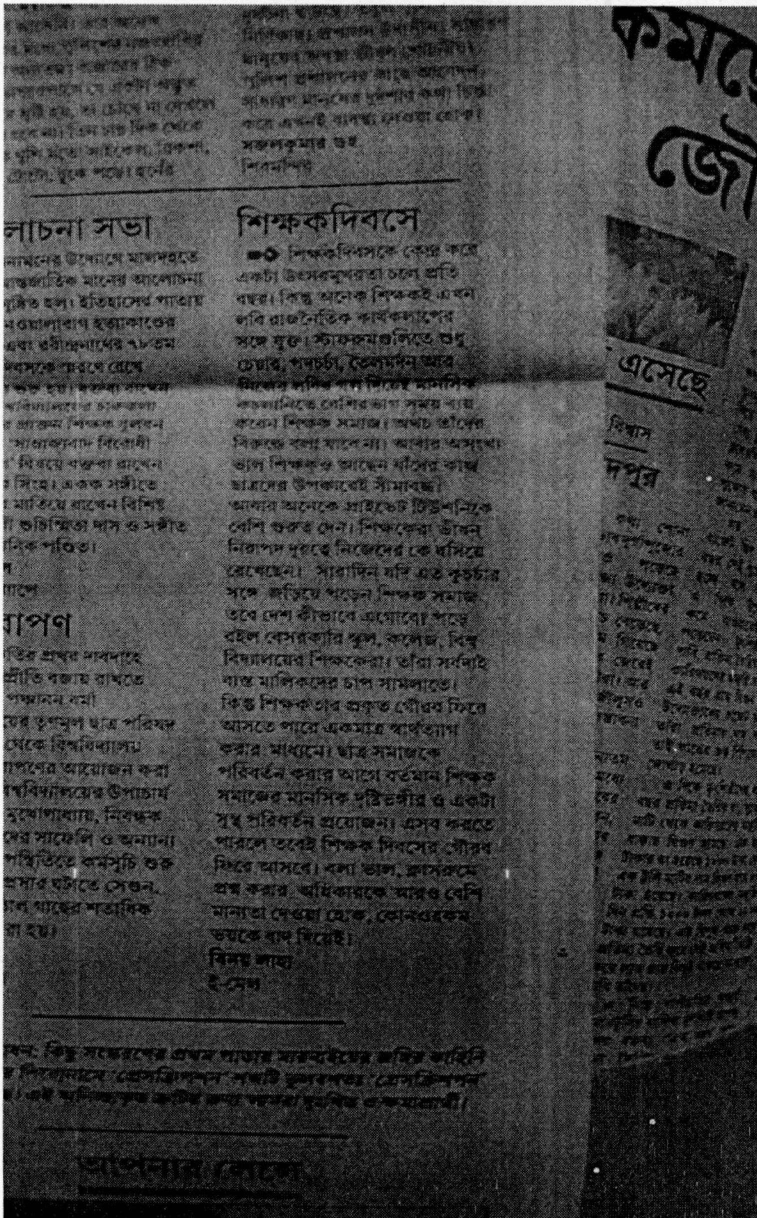

শিক্ষকদিবসে

শিক্ষকদিবসকে কেন্দ্র করে একটা উৎসবমুখরতা চলে প্রতি বছর। কিন্তু অনেক শিক্ষকই এখন দাবি রাজনৈতিক কার্যকলাপের সঙ্গে যুক্ত। স্টাফরুমগুলিতে শুধু [illegible], দলচর্চা, [illegible] আর [illegible] মানসিক [illegible] বেশির ভাগ সময় ব্যয় করেন শিক্ষক সমাজ। অথচ তাঁদের বিরুদ্ধে বলা যাবে না। আবার অসংখ্য ভাল শিক্ষকও আছেন যাঁদের কাজ ছাত্রদের উপকারেই সীমাবদ্ধ। আবার অনেকে প্রাইভেট টিউশনিকে বেশি গুরুত্ব দেন। শিক্ষকেরা তাঁদের নিরাপদ দুর্গে নিজেদেরকে বসিয়ে রেখেছেন। সারাদিন যদি এত কুচর্চার সঙ্গে জড়িয়ে পড়েন শিক্ষক সমাজ তবে দেশ কীভাবে এগোবে? পড়ে রইল বেসরকারি স্কুল, কলেজ, বিশ্ববিদ্যালয়ের শিক্ষকেরা। তাঁরা সর্বদাই ব্যস্ত মালিকদের চাপ সামলাতে। কিন্তু শিক্ষক তার প্রকৃত গৌরব ফিরে আসতে পারে একমাত্র স্বার্থত্যাগ করার মাধ্যমে। ছাত্র সমাজকে পরিবর্তন করার আগে বর্তমান শিক্ষক সমাজের মানসিক দৃষ্টিভঙ্গীর ও একটা শুদ্ধ পরিবর্তন প্রয়োজন। এসব করতে পারলে তবেই শিক্ষক দিবসের গৌরব ফিরে আসবে। বলা ভাল, ক্লাসরুমে প্রশ্ন করার অধিকারকে আরও বেশি মান্যতা দেওয়া হোক, কোনওরকম ভয়কে বাদ দিয়েই।

[illegible]

ই-মেল

■ অসচেতন: মালদহের ইংরেজবাজার পৌরবাজারে এই ভাবেই চলেছে কেনাকাটা, রবিবারেও।

চলে গেলেন এক শিক্ষাব্রতী

অন্য সব জায়গার মতো উত্তর দিনাজপুর জেলাতেও প্রবল ভাবে লেগেছে করোনার দ্বিতীয় ঢেউয়ের ধাক্কা। গত শুক্রবার মারা গেলেন রায়গঞ্জ সারদা বিদ্যামন্দির স্কুলের অন্যতম অভিজ্ঞ এক শিক্ষক। তাঁর সঙ্গে আমি ব্যক্তিগত ভাবে যুক্ত ছিলাম এক দশকের বেশি সময় ধরে। বেসরকারি শিক্ষকদের জীবনধারার মান কীভাবে উন্নত করা যায়, সে বিষয়ে দিনের পর দিন আলোচনা হয়েছে তাঁর সঙ্গে। তিনি আনন্দবাজার পত্রিকার এই বিভাগে লিখেওছিলেন বেশ কয়েকবার। জেলার বেসরকারি শিক্ষা জগতের সঙ্গে পুরো দশক যুক্ত থাকার সুবাদে জেনেছি, কী কঠোর সংগ্রাম করতে হয় বেসরকারি বিদ্যালয়ে চাকরি বাঁচানোর জন্য। দিনের পর দিন কারণে অকারণে ছাঁটাই থেকে শুরু করে নিয়ম অনুযায়ী বেতন না পাওয়াটা ছিল আমাদের নিত্যসঙ্গী। সেই নিয়ে রাস্তায় নেমে আন্দোলন ও করেছিলেন তিনি। সরকারি কর্মচারী বা শিক্ষকদের তো অনেক রকম সুবিধা থাকে মৃত্যু পরবর্তী সময়ে। এদিক থেকে বাণীব্রত ত্রিপাঠী বঞ্চিত হবেন, কারণ তিনি ছিলেন বেসরকারি শিক্ষক। তাঁর পিএফ থাকলেও তা অতি সামান্য। এই পরিস্থিতিতে তাঁর পরিবারের পাশে সিবিএসই বোর্ড দাঁড়ালে ভরসা পাবেন তাঁর পরিবার। রাজ্য সরকার বিশেষ আর্থিক প্যাকেজ দিলে খুব উপকার হতে পারে তাঁর স্ত্রী ও রেখে যাওয়া একমাত্র কন্যার। তাঁর একটি অপূর্ণ ইচ্ছা ছিল তাঁর পিএইচ ডি থিসিসটি বই হবে। তাঁর অজস্র ছাত্রছাত্রী যারা দেশ-বিদেশে প্রতিষ্ঠিত, তাঁরা সকলে মিলে বা সরকারের সহযোগিতায় তাঁর অপূর্ণ ইচ্ছা পূরণ করলে খুব ভাল হয়।

বিনয় সাহা

রায়গঞ্জ, উত্তর দিনাজপুর

সব বিভাগের জন্য লেখা/চিঠি, ই-মেল, হোয়াটসঅ্যাপ মারফত পাঠানো যাবে।

■ শিলিগুড়ির বিভিন্ন এলাকায় এভাবেই রাস্তা জুড়ে জমে থাকে জঞ্জাল। *নিজস্ব চিত্র*

শিক্ষাক্ষেত্রে দুর্নীতি

পশ্চিমবঙ্গের বেশিরভাগ বেসরকারি সিবিএসি ও আইসিএস বিদ্যালয়গুলোতে ব্যাপকভাবে দুর্নীতি জড়িয়ে রয়েছে। শিক্ষক নিয়োগ থেকে শুরু করে বেতন, পিএফ, অবসরকালীন সুবিধা নিয়ে বেশিরভাগ বিদ্যালয় উক্ত বোর্ডের বিদ্যালয়গুলির ম্যানেজমেন্ট রফা দফা করেন কাগজে কলমে। সিবিএসসির বাই ল'তে পরিষ্কারভাবে লেখা আছে যে প্রতিটি বিদ্যালয়ের শিক্ষকদের বেতন রাজ্য সরকারের মতোই হতে হবে। কে মানে? আর বাস্তবিক পক্ষে না মানলেও কাগজে কলমে দেখিয়ে দেওয়া হচ্ছে। ইদানীং প্রতিটা বিদ্যালয়ের শিক্ষকদের তালিকা বা বেতন সমস্ত কিছুই জেলার ডিআই কে জমা দিতে হয়। শিক্ষা বিভাগের আধিকারিক ডিআই কি কিছুই জানেন না? ওনার স্বাক্ষর বাদে কোনও স্কুল এনওসি পাবেন না। ইউ ডাইস দেখার দায়িত্বও ওনার। ডিআই দায়িত্ব নিয়ে বলুন উত্তর দিনাজপুর জেলার কোন বেসরকারি বিদ্যালয়ে পে কমিশন দেওয়া হয়। অথচ প্রতি বছরই বিরাট অঙ্কের বেতন দেখিয়ে শিক্ষা দফতরে পাঠিয়ে দেওয়া হয়। শিক্ষকেরা ডিআইয়ের মতো উচ্চ বেতনভোগী নন। ডিআইয়ের মতো তাঁদের চাকরি স্থায়ীও না। রাজ্যের বেকাররা এমনিই চাকরি থেকে বঞ্চিত। সরকারের ও উচিত কঠোরভাবে বেসরকারি বিদ্যালয়ের শিক্ষকদের জীবনযাত্রার মান বাড়ানো। সরকার শুধু এটা বলে খুশি থাকতে পারেন না যে সরকারি বিদ্যালয়ের শিক্ষকেরা জাতির মেরুদণ্ড। বেসরকারি বিদ্যালয়ের শিক্ষকদের ন্যায্য দাবি সরকারি স্তরে মন দিয়ে শোনা উচিত। খালি পেটে শিক্ষা দান অসম্ভব।

বিনয় লাহা
ই-মেল

খোলা-চিঠি

দার্জিলিংয়ের বিখ্যাত ... জঙ্গল দাবানলে ভস্মীভূত হওয়ার খবর শুধুই ভয়ের ইঙ্গিত দেয়। অসংখ্য নামীদামি গাছগাছালি ও অসংখ্য ... থেকে প্রাণে বাঁচতে এবং খাবারের সন্ধানে। আজকাল এই গুরুত্বপূর্ণ খবরগুলি নিয়ে মানুষের ভাবনা চিন্তায় কোনওরকম উত্তাপ নেই। এসব ভুলে শুধুই চিন্তা, কে কীভাবে ...

বেহাল রাস্তা

[illegible]

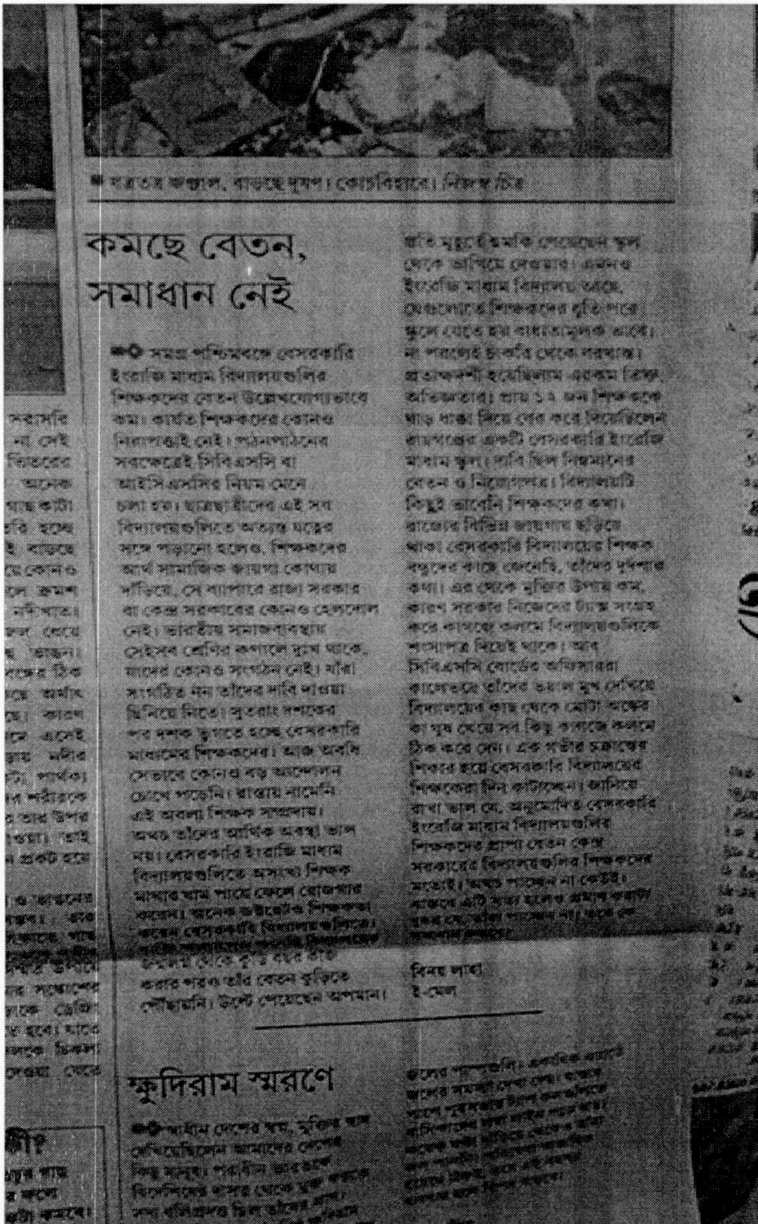

কমছে বেতন, সমাধান নেই

ক্ষুদিরাম স্মরণে

ডেঙ্গি রুখতে স্মোক-গান নিয়ে প্রশাসনিক তৎপরতা। শিলিগুড়িতে।

তথ্যে ভরা সিলেবাস

সিবিএসসি বোর্ডের একাদশ এবং দ্বাদশ শ্রেণির ইতিহাস পাঠ্যবইটি শুধুমাত্র জটিল তথ্য ও অত্যধিক ইংরেজি ভাষার জটিলতায় পুষ্ট করা হয়েছে। এক্সপার্ট কমিটিতে সারা ভারতের নামী বিশ্ববিদ্যালয়গুলির শিক্ষকেরা রয়েছেন। আদতে একাদশ ও দ্বাদশ শ্রেণির মানের তুলনায় বেশি উচ্চ মানের ভাষা, জটিলতা, ও সিলেবাসের ধারাবাহিক সংযুক্তিকরণের অভাবে পাঠ্যপুস্তকটি পড়তে আগ্রহ পাচ্ছে না অধিকাংশ পড়ুয়া। অগত্যা সোজাসাপটা গাইড বুকের দিকেই যেতে বাধ্য হচ্ছে। এটা চিরাচরিত সত্য যে, গাইড বই ও নোটস পড়ার ফলে নম্বর ভাল উঠছে বটে, তবে বিষয়ের গভীরতা কতটা থাকছে, সে ব্যাপারে সন্দেহ রয়ে যাচ্ছে। উত্তর দিনাজপুর জেলার বেশ কিছু সিবিএসসি স্কুলের তথ্য সংগ্রহ করতে গিয়ে দেখা যায় যে, অনেকেই নব্বইয়ের উপর নম্বর পেয়েছে বিভিন্ন বিষয়ে। এমনকি, একশোয় একশো পেয়েছে ইতিহাসের মতো বিষয়েও। কিন্তু তাদের সঙ্গে কথা বলে জানতে পেরেছি যে, পাঠ্যপুস্তকের থেকে গাইডবই অনেক বেশি মূল্যবান। বইয়ের আমূল পরিবর্তন দরকার।

বিনয় লাহা
ই-মেল

বেহাল রাস্তা

কোথাও রাস্তার পিচ উঠে গিয়েছে। কোথাও জল জমেছে। ৩১ নম্বর জাতীয় সড়কের কিছু অংশের এমনই অবস্থা। প্রায় দু'বছর আগে অংশটি সংস্কার করা হয়েছিল। কিন্তু তা ভেঙে গিয়েছে। ভাঙা রাস্তায় বালি পাথর দেওয়া হলেও বৃষ্টি হওয়ার সঙ্গে সঙ্গে সেই বালি-পাথর ধুয়ে গিয়েছে। এলাকায় একাধিক স্কুল রয়েছে। সমস্যায় পড়ছে ছাত্রছাত্রীরা। গর্তগুলি জলে ভরে থাকলে অনেক সময় সেগুলি দেখা যায় না। তখন দুর্ঘটনা ঘটে। সমস্যা হচ্ছে রোগীদেরও।

এলাকায় প্রতি বছর নানা রোগ দেখা দেয়। বিষয়টির সমাধান চাই

বিকাশ পাল
করণদিঘি

জঞ্জাল যন্ত্রণা

জাতীয় সড়কের দু'পাশ ভরে গিয়েছে জঞ্জালের স্তূপে। এই স্তূপ পেরিয়েই প্রতিদিন বাস, অটো, টোটো চলাচল করে। ডাম্পিং গ্রাউন্ডের কোনও ব্যবস্থা নেই। মূলত বাজার এলাকাগুলির আবর্জনা জাতীয় সড়কের ধারে ফেলা হচ্ছে। দুর্গন্ধে অতিষ্ঠ বাসিন্দারা। আবর্জনা পেরিয়েই

জল অপচয়। রায়গঞ্জে।

চাপ বাড়ছে শিক্ষকদের

উত্তর দিনাজপুর জেলার কমবেশি সব বেসরকারি ইংরেজি মাধ্যম বিদ্যালয়গুলিতে শিক্ষকদের উপর চাপ বাড়িয়ে চলেছেন কর্তৃপক্ষ। কোনও বিদ্যালয়ে ধুতি পড়তে হয় শিক্ষকদের, কোনও বিদ্যালয়ে টাই পড়তে হয় জোর জবরদস্তি ভাবে। কোনও কোনও বিদ্যালয়ে মোবাইল ব্যবহার করতে দেওয়া হয় না। অথচ ম্যানেজমেন্টের সব লোকই মোবাইল ব্যবহার করেন। তাঁরা তো ধুতি বা টাই পরে আসেন না। শিক্ষকদের উপর নির্যাতনের মাত্রা এতটাই বেশি যে, কোনও শিক্ষক ভয়ে মুখ খোলেন না। মুখ খুললেই চাকরি হারানোর আশঙ্কা প্রবল। একবিংশ শতাব্দীতে দাঁড়িয়ে এই শিক্ষকদের আর কত হেনস্থা হতে হবে? সম্প্রতি একটি স্কুলে ফতোয়া জারি করা হয়েছে শিক্ষকদের মোবাইল ব্যবহার করা নিয়ে। যে সব বিদ্যালয়ে শিক্ষকদের উপর এত নির্যাতন চালাচ্ছে, সেখানে উত্তর দিনাজপুর জেলা শিক্ষা দফতর ও প্রশাসন এত নীরব কেন? কোনও বিদ্যালয়ে সরকারি স্কেলে বেতন দেওয়া হয় না। গায়ের জোর দেখিয়ে বিদ্যালয় চালানোকে মদত দিচ্ছে সিবিএসসি এবং আইসিএসসি বোর্ড। শ্রম দফতর নাকে তেল দিয়ে ঘুমাচ্ছে, এসআই এবং ডিআইরা শিক্ষকদের সঙ্গে কথা বলছেন না। তাঁরা ভয় পেলে পুলিশের সাহায্যে বিদ্যালয়গুলিকে জেরা করুক। উত্তর দিনাজপুর জেলার ইংরেজি শিক্ষার ইতিহাস রয়েছে প্রায় ৪২ বছরের। এই ইতিহাস যাতে আর কালিমালিপ্ত না হয় এবং শিক্ষকেরা যাতে নিরাপত্তা নিয়ে পড়াতে পারেন, তাঁর দায়িত্ব নিতে হবে জেলা ও রাজ্য শিক্ষা দফতর ও দিল্লির সিবিএসসি ও মানব উন্নয়ন দফতরকে। বিপুল অংশের বেসরকারি বিদ্যালয়গুলির শিক্ষকেরা যে যন্ত্রণা নিয়ে ধারাবাহিক ভাবে শিক্ষা দান করে চলেছেন, তাঁদের ভবিষ্যত কোথায়?

বিনয় সাহা

ই-মেল

বেতন প্রসঙ্গে

■নিষেধ সত্ত্বেও চলছে বালিতোলা। সেবকের তিস্তা নদীতে। *নিজস্ব চিত্র*

বেতন-বৈষম্য, শিক্ষকের দুর্ভোগ

পশ্চিমবঙ্গের বেশিরভাগ বেসরকারি বিদ্যালয়গুলিতে শিক্ষকদের কোনও নিরাপত্তা নেই। নিয়োগপত্র দেওয়া হয় না বেশিরভাগ ক্ষেত্রেই। বেতন নিয়ম বহির্ভূত ভাবে দেওয়া হয়। চাকরি থেকে বরখাস্ত করতে ম্যানেজম্যান্টের মুখের কথাই শেষ কথা। এ ব্যাপারে শিক্ষা দফতর যেমন উদাসীন ঠিক তেমনই উদাসীন শ্রম দফতর। এই সব স্কুলের শিক্ষকদের বেতন ন্যায্যভাবে দেখভালের দায়িত্ব কেন্দ্র ও রাজ্য সরকারের। কেন্দ্র সরকার বিদ্যালয়গুলির অনুমোদন দিলেও রাজ্য সরকারের কাছ থেকে নো অবজেকশন শংসাপত্র নিতে হয় বিদ্যালয়গুলিকে। বেসরকারি বিদ্যালয়ের শিক্ষক ও সরকারি বিদ্যালয়ের বেতন পরিকাঠামোর কোনও তফাত নেই। তবে ব্যবহারিক ভাবে বেসরকারি বিদ্যালয়ের শিক্ষকদের বেতন খামখেয়ালিপনায় পরিপূর্ণ। শিক্ষকদের ন্যায্য অধিকার পিএফ। সেটা অধিকাংশ স্কুলে নেই। আর যে সব স্কুলে আছে, তার পরিমাণ খুবই কম। সরকারের কাছে বিশেষ অনুরোধ যেন এই সব বেসরকারী বিদ্যালয়ের শিক্ষকরা একটা ভাল বেতন পান।

বিনয় লাহা
রায়গঞ্জ

ভাঙন আতঙ্ক

মালদহ জেলার মানিকচক ব্লকের কালিন্দ্রী নদীর পাড় ধরে যে রাস্তা গিয়েছে, তা নদীগর্ভে যাওয়ার উপক্রম হয়েছে। এই বর্ষায় সে আশঙ্কা অহরহ সংলগ্ন গ্রামবাসীদের কুরে কুরে খাচ্ছে। রাস্তা নদী খেয়ে ফেললে কী পরিস্থিতির সৃষ্টি হতে পারে, তা সহজেই আন্দাজ করা যায়। নদীর পাড়ের এই রাস্তা ব্যবহার করেন [illegible], ছোট [illegible], [illegible], [illegible], [illegible], [illegible], [illegible], গোবিন্দপুর প্রভৃতি গ্রামের লক্ষাধিক মানুষ। এই রাস্তা নির্মাণের সঙ্গে তাঁদের আবেগও জড়িয়ে আছে। বহু বছর ধরে আবেদন-নিবেদন করে প্রধানমন্ত্রী গ্রাম সড়ক যোজনায় তাঁরা এই রাস্তা পেয়েছে মাত্র বছর দুই-তিন আগে। রাস্তা বাঁচানোর জন্য গ্রামবাসীরা জেলাশাসক, বিডিও, সেচ দফতর সবার দ্বারস্থ হয়েছেন। কিন্তু সরকারি উদ্যোগ চোখে পড়েনি। বালির বস্তা দিয়ে গ্রামের লোকেরা ভাঙন রোধের চেষ্টা করেছেন। কিন্তু সংশয় রয়েছে এলাকাবাসীর।

সাগর মণ্ডল
মালদহ

LETTERS TO THE EDITOR

The reckless

SIR, The industrial scenario in West Bengal gets bleaker still with the killing of Hare Krishna Maheswari, CEO of North Brook jute mill in Hooghly district. Trade union leaders are becoming increasingly reckless and now, as it turns out, murderous as well. Is there a political conspiracy? The parties are blaming each other in an exercise in mutual mud-slinging.

The jute industry has been in crisis for quite some time. The mill worker might be apprehensive over reduction of working hours. He fears that in due course of time, he might become jobless. From the CPI-M's misadventure in Singur to the closure of Hind Motors under the Trinamul Congress, the industrial trend in West Bengal has been consistently distressing. There is increasing insecurity at the level of the corporate management. The culprits deserve exemplary punishment.

Yours, etc., Binay Laha,
Kishanganj (Bihar).

CAUVERY JUSTICE

SIR, We are shocked to learn that the Centre intends to set up the Cauvery Management

CORONA HITS GLOBAL EDUCATION

Binay Laha

Putting a rave upon my write up on the impact of covid -19 upon education has not been palpable for many months as the education sector having suffered even today globally.

Worst effected is the public sector of education in the third world country where providing internet is a soul challenge for the school, college or for the university. Actually it is really difficult to go for offline classes as gathering may increase civid rapidly. So the choice is online or virtual classes. But at the same time only virtual classes can not be a substitute for offline classes, it may be mere attachment to studies.

The urban platform of education in the third world countries may knock to be smart, but surely not smartest tie up with the common agenda of demand. The first World countries are having online classes structure from the pro corona period. They have put no extra challenges. The rural mode of education has faced the severe problems for months. Internet facilities are a dream to the students of the remote villages of India, Bangladesh, Pakistan, Nepal or in Bhutan. It has totally been stopped either for crisis of infrastructure or for any good will to promote it.

Long six to seven months there were indeed no classes held in the government sector of education in India and different other countries. Corona period has clearly put a barrier in between have and the have not. But the situation in the private sector of education has been progressing since the day the lock down has been declared, but it was also for limited number of schools because maximum number of students in private institutions belong to "have " categories. Though their parents face monetary problems during this fatal problems for months. Overall it failed to balance.

In some institutions which are located in the urban areas they have practically created whatsapp group and conducted classes through zoom meet or through google meet. But many number of students have lost attention to attend it for a long period of time. Some how the private sector of education is still managing as there is no other substitute to continue education. Government sectors of education were as sluggish as before.

They pretend to continue but failed to implement. If the problems of the First World countries in continuing education are less but it is not easy for them to pull all students in the same flow.

Monetary trasanction have fallen globally so in turn it failed to fructify education sector too. But now a days the situation is bit changing. The reality is that the government sector is also trying to compete with the private sector of education specially in India. Covid is still putting it's paw upon the freedom of the people of the globe. Apart from many negativity of Covid ,it has many positive outcome. It has revealed the common goal of life.

It has shown the expertisation of the private sector, albeit many other challenges like non payment or half payment. At the same time it has created a new culture of 'Work from Home'.

Last but not the least it is too include that surviving a life is far important rather than institutional education and acquiring mere degrees.

The writer is a freelancer and the editor of Indology Magazine.

May be reached at -[illegible]

Macaulay's Minute on Education, February 2, 1835

Minute by the Hon'ble T. B. Macaulay, dated the 2nd February 1835.

As it seems to be the opinion of some of the gentlemen who compose the Committee of Public Instruction that the course which they have hitherto pursued was strictly prescribed by the British Parliament in 1813 and as, if that opinion be correct, a legislative act will be necessary to warrant a change, I have thought it right to refrain from taking any part in the preparation of the adverse statements which are now before us, and to reserve what I had to say on the subject till it should come before me as a Member of the Council of India.

It does not appear to me that the Act of Parliament can by any art of contraction be made to bear the meaning which has been assigned to it. It contains nothing about the particular languages or sciences which are to be studied. A sum is set apart "for the revival and promotion of literature, and the encouragement of the learned natives of India, and for the introduction and promotion of a knowledge of the sciences among the inhabitants of the British territories." It is argued, or rather taken for granted, that by literature the Parliament can have meant only Arabic and Sanscrit literature; that they never would have given the honourable appellation of "a learned native" to a native who was familiar with the poetry of Milton, the metaphysics of Locke, and the physics of Newton; but that they meant to designate by that name only such persons as might have studied in the sacred books of the Hindoos all the uses of cusa-grass, and all the mysteries of absorption into the Deity. This does not appear to be a very satisfactory interpretation. To take a parallel case: Suppose that the Pacha of Egypt, a country once superior inknowledge to the nations of Europe, but now sunk far below them, were to appropriate a sum for the purpose "of reviving and promoting literature, and encouraging learned natives of Egypt," would any body infer that he meant the youth of his Pachalik to give years to the study of hieroglyphics, to search into all the doctrines disguised under the fable of Osiris, and to ascertain with all possible accuracy the ritual with which cats and onions were anciently adored? Would he be justly charged with inconsistency if, instead of employing his young subjects in deciphering obelisks, he were to order them to be instructed in the English and French languages, and in all the sciences to which those languages are the chief keys?

The words on which the supporters of the old system rely do not bear them out, and other words follow which seem to be quite decisive on the other side. This lakh of rupees is set apart not only for "reviving literature in India," the phrase on which their whole interpretation is founded, but also "for the introduction and promotion of a knowledge of the sciences among the inhabitants of the British territories"-words which are alone sufficient to authorize all the changes for which I contend.

If the Council agree in my construction no legislative act will be necessary. If they differ from me, I will propose a short act rescinding that I clause of the Charter of 1813 from which the difficulty arises.

The argument which I have been considering affects only the form of proceeding. But the admirers of the oriental system of education have used another argument, which, if we admit it to be valid, is decisive against all change. They conceive that the public faith is pledged to the present system, and that to alter the appropriation of any of the funds which have hitherto been spent in encouraging the study of Arabic and Sanscrit would be downright spoliation. It is not easy to understand by what process of reasoning they can have arrived at this conclusion. The grants which are made from the public purse for the encouragement of literature differ in no respect from the grants which are made from the same purse for other objects of real or supposed utility. We found a sanitarium on a spot which we suppose tobe healthy. Do we thereby pledge ourselves to keep a sanitarium there if the result should not answer our expectations? We commence the erection of a pier. Is it a violation of the public faith to stop the works, if we afterwards see reason to believe that the building will be useless? The rights of property are undoubtedly sacred. But nothing endangers those rights so much as the practice, now unhappily too common, of attributing them to things to which they do not belong. Those who would impart to abuses the sanctity of property are in truth imparting to the institution of property the unpopularity and the fragility of abuses. If the Government has given to any person a formal assurance-nay, if the Government has excited in any person's mind a reasonable expectation-that he shall receive a certain income as a teacher or a learner of Sanscrit or Arabic, I would respect that person's pecuniary interests. I would rather err on the side of liberality to individuals than suffer the public faith to be called in question. But to talk of a Government pledging itself to teach certain languages and certain sciences, though those languages may become useless, though those sciences may be exploded, seems to me quite unmeaning. There is not a single word in any public instrument from which it can be inferred that the Indian Government ever intended to give any pledge on this subject, or ever considered the destination of these funds as unalterably fixed. But, had it been otherwise, I should have denied the competence of our predecessors to bind us by any pledge on such a subject. Suppose that a Government had in the last century enacted in the most solemn manner that all its subjects should, to the end of time, be inoculated for the small-pox, would that Government be bound to persist in the practice after Jenner's discovery? These promises of which nobody claims the performance, and from which nobody can grant a release, these vested rights which vest in nobody, this property without proprietors, this robbery which makes nobody poorer, may be comprehended by persons of higher faculties than mine. I consider this plea merely as a set form of words, regularly used both in England and in India, in defenceof every abuse for which no other plea can be setup.

I hold this lakh of rupees to be quite at the disposal of the Governor-General in Council for the purpose of promoting learning in India in any way which may be thought most advisable. I hold his Lordship to be quite as free to direct that it shall no longer be employed in encouraging Arabic and Sanscrit, as he is to direct that the reward for killing tigers in Mysore shall be diminished, or that no more public money shall be expended on the chaunting at the cathedral.

We now come to the gist of the matter. We have a fund to be employed as Government shall direct for the intellectual improvement of the people of this country. The simple question is, what is the most useful way of employing it?

All parties seem to be agreed on one point, that the dialects commonly spoken among the natives of this part of India contain neither literary nor scientific information, and are moreover so poor and rude that, until they are enriched from some other quarter, it will not be easy to translate any valuable work into them. It seems to be admitted on all sides, that the intellectual improvement of those classes of the people who have the means of pursuing higher studies can at present be affected only by means of some language not vernacular amongstthem.

What then shall that language be? One-half of the committee maintain that it should be the English. The other half strongly recommend the Arabic and Sanscrit. The whole question seems to me to be-which language is the best worth knowing?

I have no knowledge of either Sanscrit or Arabic. But I have done what I could to form a correct estimate of their value. I have read translations of the most celebrated Arabic and Sanscrit works. I have conversed, both here and at home, with men distinguished by their proficiency in the Eastern tongues. I am quite ready to take the oriental learning at the valuation of the orientalists themselves. I have never found one among them who could deny that a single shelf of a good European library was worth the whole native literature of India and Arabia. The intrinsic superiority of the Western literature is indeed fully admitted by those members of the committee who support the oriental plan of education.

It will hardly be disputed, I suppose, that the department of literature in which the Eastern writers stand highest is poetry. And I certainly never met with any orientalist who ventured to maintain that the Arabic and Sanscrit poetry could be compared to that of the great European nations. But when we pass from works of imagination to works in which facts are recorded and general principles investigated, the superiority of the Europeans becomes absolutely immeasurable. It is, I believe, no exaggeration to say that all the historical information which has been collected from all the books written in the Sanscrit language is less valuable than what may be found in the most paltry abridgments used at preparatory schools in England. In every branch of physical or moral philosophy, the relative position of the two nations is nearly the same.

How then stands the case? We have to educate a people who cannot at present be educated by means of their mother-tongue. We must teach them some foreign language. The claims of our own language it is hardly necessary to recapitulate. It stands pre- eminent even among the languages of the West. It abounds with works of imagination not inferior to the noblest which Greece has bequeathed to us,-with models of every species of eloquence,-with historical composition, which, considered merely as narratives, have seldom been surpassed, and which, considered as vehicles of ethical and political instruction, have never been equaled-with just and lively representations of human life and human nature,-with the most profound speculations on metaphysics, morals, government, jurisprudence, trade,-with full and correct information respecting every experimental science which tends to preserve the health, to increase the comfort, or to expand the intellect of man. Whoever knows that language has ready access to all the vast intellectual wealth which all the wisest nations of the earth have created and hoarded in the course of ninety generations. It may safely be said that the literature now extant in

that language is of greater value than all the literature which three hundred years ago was extant in all the languages of the world together. Nor is this all. In India, English is the language spoken by the ruling class. It is spoken by the higher class of natives at the seats of Government. It is likely to become the language of commerce throughout the seas of the East. It is the language of two great European communities which are rising, the one in the south of Africa, the other in Australia,-communities which are every year becoming more important and more closely connected with our Indian empire. Whether we look at the intrinsic value of our literature, or at the particular situation of thiscountry, we shall see the strongest reason to think that, of all foreign tongues, the English tongue is that which would be the most useful to our nativesubjects.

The question now before us is simply whether, when it is in our power to teach this language, we shall teach languages in which, by universal confession, there are no books on any subject which deserve to be compared to our own, whether, when we can teach European science, we shall teach systems which, by universal confession, wherever they differ from those of Europe differ for the worse, and whether, when we can patronize sound philosophy and true history, we shall countenance, at the public expense, medical doctrines which would disgrace an English farrier, astronomy which would move laughter in girls at an English boarding school, history abounding with kings thirty feet high and reigns thirty thousand years long, and geography made of seas of treacle and seas ofbutter.

We are not without experience to guide us. History furnishes several analogous cases, and they all teach the same lesson. There are, in modern times, to go no further, two memorable instances of a great impulse given to the mind of a whole society, of prejudices overthrown, of knowledge diffused, of taste purified, of arts and sciences planted in countries which had recently been ignorant and barbarous.

The first instance to which I refer is the great revival of letters among the Western nations at the close of the fifteenth and the beginning of the sixteenth century. At that time almost everything that was worth reading was contained in the writings of the ancient Greeks and Romans. Had our ancestors acted as the Committee of Public Instruction has hitherto noted, had they neglected the language of Thucydides and Plato, and the language of Cicero and Tacitus, had they confined their attention to the old dialects of our own island, had they printed nothing and taught nothing at the universities but chronicles in Anglo-Saxon and romances in Norman French,-would England ever have been what she now is? What the Greek and Latin were to the contemporaries of More and Ascham, our tongue is to the people of India. The literature of England is now more valuable than that of classical antiquity. I doubt whether the Sanscrit literature be as valuable as that of our Saxon and Norman progenitors. In some departments-in history for example-I am certain that it is much lessso.

Another instance may be said to be still before our eyes. Within the last hundred and twenty years, a nation which had previously been in a state as barbarous as that in which our ancestors were before the Crusades has gradually emerged from the ignorance in which it was sunk, and has taken its place among civilized communities. I speak of Russia. There is now in that country a large educated class abounding with persons fit to serve the State in the highest functions, and in nowise inferior to the most accomplished men who adorn the best circles of Paris and London. There is reason to hope that this vast empire which, in the time of our grandfathers, was probably behind the Punjab, may in the time of our grandchildren, be pressing close on France and Britain in the career of improvement. And how was this change effected? Not by flattering national prejudices; not by feeding the mind of the young Muscovite with the old women's stories which his rude fathers had believed; not by filling his head with lying legends about St. Nicholas; not by encouraging him to study the great question, whether the world was or not created on the 13th of September; not by calling him "a learned native" when he had mastered all these points of knowledge; but by teaching him those foreign languages in which the greatest mass of information had been laid up, and thus putting all that information within his reach. The languages of western Europe civilised Russia. I cannot doubt that they will do for the Hindoo what they have done for theTartar.

And what are the arguments against that course which seems to be alike recommended by theory and by experience? It is said that we ought to secure the co- operation of the native public, and that we can do this only by teaching Sanscrit and Arabic.

I can by no means admit that, when a nation of high intellectual attainments undertakes to superintend the education of a nation comparatively ignorant, the learners are absolutely to prescribe the course which is to be taken by the teachers. It is not necessary however to say anything on this subject. For it is proved by unanswerable evidence, that we are not at present securing the co-operation of the natives. It would be bad enough to consult their intellectual taste at the expense of their intellectual health. But we are consulting neither. We are withholding from them the learning which is palatable to them. We are forcing on them the mock learning which theynauseate.

This is proved by the fact that we are forced to pay our Arabic and Sanscrit students while those who learn English are willing to pay us. All the declamations in the world about the love and reverence of the natives for their sacred dialects will never, in the mind of any impartial person, outweigh this undisputed fact, that we cannot find in all our vast empire a single student who will let us teach him those dialects, unless we will pay him.

I have now before me the accounts of the Mudrassa for one month, the month of December, 1833. The Arabic students appear to have been seventy-seven in number. All receive stipends from the public. The whole amount paid to them is above 500 rupees a month. On the other side of the account stands the following item:

Deduct amount realized from the out-students of English for the months of May, June, and July last-103 rupees.

I have been told that it is merely from want of local experience that I am surprised at these phenomena, and that it is not the fashion for students in India to study at their own charges. This only confirms me in my opinions. Nothing is more certain than that it never can in any part of the world be necessary to pay men for doing what they think pleasant or profitable. India is no exception to this rule. The people of India do not require to be paid for eating rice when they are hungry, or for wearing woollen cloth in the cold season. To come nearer to the case before us:-The children who learn their letters and a little elementary arithmetic from the village schoolmaster are not paid by him. He is paid for teaching them. Why then is it necessary to pay people to learn Sanscrit and Arabic? Evidently because it is universally felt that the Sanscrit and Arabic are languages the knowledge of which does not compensate for the trouble of acquiring them. On all such subjects the state of the market is the detective test.

Other evidence is not wanting, if other evidence were required. A petition was presented last year to the committee by several ex-students of the Sanscrit College. The petitioners stated that they had studied in the college ten or twelve years, that they had made themselves acquainted with Hindoo literature and science, that they had received certificates of proficiency. And what is the fruit of all this? "Notwithstanding such testimonials," they say, "we have but little prospect of bettering our condition without the kind assistance of your honourable committee, the indifference with which we are generally looked upon by our countrymen leaving no hope of encouragement and assistance from them." They therefore beg that they may be recommended to the Governor-General for places under the Government-not places of high dignity or emolument, but such as may just enable them to exist. "We want means," they say, "for a decent living, and for our progressive improvement, which, however, we cannot obtain without the assistance of Government, by whom we have been educated and maintained from childhood." They conclude by representing very pathetically that they are sure that itwas never the intention of Government, after behaving so liberally to them during their education, to abandon them to destitution andneglect.

I have been used to see petitions to Government for compensation. All those petitions, even the most unreasonable of them, proceeded on the supposition that some loss had been sustained, that some wrong had been inflicted. These are surely the first petitioners who ever demanded compensation for having been educated gratis, for having been supported by the public during twelve years, and then sent forth into the world well furnished with literature and science. They represent their education as an injury which gives them a claim on the Government for redress, as an injury for which the stipends paid to them during the infliction were a very inadequate compensation. And I doubt not that they are in the right. They have wasted the best years of life in learning what procures for them neither bread nor respect. Surely we might with advantage have saved the cost of making these persons useless and miserable. Surely, men may be brought up to be burdens to the public and objects of contempt to their neighbours at a somewhat smaller charge to the State. But such is our policy. We do not even stand neuter in the contest between truth and falsehood. We are not content to leave the natives to the influence of their own hereditary prejudices. To the natural difficulties which obstruct the progress of sound science in the East, we add great difficulties of our own making. Bounties and premiums, such as ought not to be given even for the propagation of truth, we lavish on false texts and falsephilosophy.

By acting thus we create the very evil which we fear. We are making that opposition which we do not find. What we spend on the Arabic and Sanscrit Colleges is not merely a dead loss to the cause of truth. It is bounty-money paid to raise up champions of error. It goes to form a nest not merely of helpless placehunters but of bigots prompted alike by passion and by interest to raise a cry against every useful scheme of education. If there should be any opposition among the natives to the change which I recommend, that opposition will be the effect of our own system. It will be headed by persons supported by our stipends and trained in our colleges. The longer we persevere in our present course, the more formidable will that opposition be. It will be every year reinforced by recruits whom we are paying. From the native society, leftto itself, we have no difficulties to apprehend. All the murmuring will come from that oriental interest which we have, by artificial means, called into being and nursed intostrength.

There is yet another fact which is alone sufficient to prove that the feeling of the native public, when left to itself, is not such as the supporters of the old system represent it to be. The committee have thought fit to lay out above a lakh of rupees in printing Arabic and Sanscrit books. Those books find no purchasers. It is very rarely that a single copy is disposed of. Twenty-three thousand volumes, most of them folios and quartos, fill the libraries or rather the lumber-rooms of this body. The committee contrive to get rid of some portion of their vast stock of oriental literature by giving books away. But they cannot give so fast as they print. About twenty thousand rupees a year are spent in adding fresh masses of waste paper to a hoard which, one should think, is already sufficiently ample. During the last three years about sixty thousand rupees have been expended in this manner. The sale of Arabic and Sanscrit books during those three years has not yielded quite one thousand rupees. In the meantime, the School Book Society is selling seven or eight thousand English volumes every year, and not only pays the expenses of printing but realizes a profit of twenty per cent. on its outlay.

The fact that the Hindoo law is to be learned chiefly from Sanscrit books, and the Mahometan law from Arabic books, has been much insisted on, but seems not to bear at all on the question. We are commanded by Parliament to ascertain and digest the laws of India. The assistance of a Law Commission has been given to us for that purpose. As soon as the Code is promulgated the Shastersand the Hedaya will be useless to a moonsiff or a Sudder Ameen. I hope and trust that, before the boys who are now entering at the Mudrassa and the Sanscrit College have completed their studies, this great work will be finished. It would be manifestly absurd to educate the rising generation with a view to a state of things which we mean to alter before they reachmanhood.

But there is yet another argument which seems even more untenable. It is said that the Sanscrit and the Arabic are the languages in which the sacred books of a hundred millions of people are written, and that they are on that account entitled to peculiar encouragement. Assuredly it is the duty of the British Government in India to be not only tolerant but neutral on all religious questions. But to encourage the study of a literature, admitted to be of small intrinsic value, only because that literature inculcated the most serious errors on the most important subjects, is a course hardly reconcilable with reason, with morality, or even with that very neutrality which ought, as we all agree, to be sacredly preserved. It is confined that a language is barren of useful knowledge. We are to teach it because it is fruitful of monstrous superstitions. We are to teach false history, false astronomy, false medicine, because we find them in company with a false religion.

We abstain, and I trust shall always abstain, from giving any public encouragement to those who are engaged in the work of converting the natives to Christianity. And while we act thus, can we reasonably or decently bribe men, out of the revenues of the State, to waste their youth in learning how they are to purify themselves after touching an ass or what texts of the Vedas they are to repeat to expiate the crime of killing agoat?

It is taken for granted by the advocates of oriental learning that no native of this country can possibly attain more than a mere smattering of English. They do not attempt to prove this. But they perpetually insinuate it. They designate the education which their opponents recommend as a mere spelling-book education. They assume it as undeniable that the question is between a profound knowledge of Hindoo and Arabian literature and science on the one side, and superficial knowledge of the rudiments of English on the other. This is not merely an assumption, but an assumption contrary to all reason and experience. We know that foreigners of all nations do learn our language sufficiently to have access to all the most abstruse knowledge which it contains sufficiently to relish even the more delicate graces of our most idiomatic writers. There are in this very town natives who are quite competent to discuss political or scientific questions with fluency and precision in the English language. I have heard the very question on which I am now writing discussed by native gentlemen with a liberality and an intelligence which would do credit to any member of the Committee of Public Instruction. Indeedit is unusual to find, even in the literary circles of the Continent, any foreigner who can express himself in English with so much facility and correctness as we find in many Hindoos. Nobody, I suppose, will contend that English is so difficult to a Hindoo as Greek to an Englishman. Yet an intelligent English youth, in a much smaller number of years than our unfortunate pupils pass at the Sanscrit College, becomes able to read, to enjoy, and even to imitate not unhappily the compositions of the best Greek authors. Less than half the time which enables an English youth to read Herodotus and Sophocles ought to enable a Hindoo to read Hume and Milton.

To sum up what I have said. I think it clear that we are not fettered by the Act of Parliament of 1813, that we are not fettered by any pledge expressed or implied, that we are free to employ our funds as we choose, that we ought to employ them in teaching what is best worth knowing, that English is better worth knowing than Sanscrit or Arabic, that the natives are desirous to be taught English, and are not desirous to be taught Sanscrit or Arabic, that neither as the languages of law nor as the languages of religion have the Sanscritand Arabic any peculiar claim to our encouragement, that it is possible to make natives of this country thoroughly good English scholars, and that to this end our efforts ought to bedirected.

In one point I fully agree with the gentlemen to whose general views I am opposed. I feel with them that it is impossible for us, with our limited means, to attempt to educate the body of the people. We must at present do our best to form a class who may be interpreters between us and the millions whom we govern, -a class of persons Indian in blood and colour, but English in tastes, in opinions, in morals and in intellect. To that class we may leave it to refine the vernacular dialects of the country, to enrich those dialects with terms of science borrowed from the Western nomenclature, and to render them by degrees fit vehicles for conveying knowledge to the great mass of the population.

I would strictly respect all existing interests. I would deal even generously with all individuals who have had fair reason to expect a pecuniary provision. But I would strike at the root of the bad system which has hitherto been fostered by us. I would at once stop the printing of Arabic and Sanscrit books. I would abolish the Mudrassa and the Sanscrit College at Calcutta. Benares is the great seat of Brahminical learning; Delhi of Arabic learning. If we retain the Sanscrit College at Bonares and the Mahometan College at Delhi we do enough and much more than enough in my opinion, for the Eastern languages. If the Benares and Delhi Colleges should be retained, I would at least recommend that no stipends shall be given to any students who may hereafter repair thither, but that the people shall be left to make their own choice between the rival systems of education without being bribed by us to learn what they have no desire to know. The funds which would thus be placed at our disposal would enable us to give larger encouragement to the Hindoo College at Calcutta, and establish in the principal cities throughout the Presidencies of Fort William and Agra schools in which the English language might be well and thoroughly taught.

If the decision of His Lordship in Council should be such as I anticipate, I shallenter on the performance of my duties with the greatest zeal and alacrity. If, on the other hand, it be the opinion of the Government that the present system ought to remain unchanged, I beg that I may be permitted to retire from the chair of the Committee. I feel that I could not be of the smallest use there. I feel also that I should be lending my countenance to what I firmly believe to be a mere delusion. I believe that the present system tends not to accelerate the progress of truth but to delay the natural death of expiring errors. I conceive that we have at present no right to the respectable name of a Board of Public Instruction. We are a Board for wasting the public money, for printing books which are of less value than the paper on which they are printed was while it was blank-for giving artificial encouragement to absurd history, absurd metaphysics, absurd physics, absurd theology-for raising up a breed of scholars who find their scholarship an incumbrance and blemish, who live on the public while they are receiving their education, and whose education is so utterly useless to them that, when they have received it, they must either starve or live on the public all the rest of their lives. Entertaining these opinions, I am naturally desirous to decline all share in the responsibility of a body which, unless it alters its whole mode of proceedings, I must consider, not merely as useless, but as positively noxious.

ANNEXURE-I

Appointment, Service Conditions and Duties of the Teachers in CBSE Affiliated Schools

1. Qualification of the Teacher:

a. Sec. 23 of RTE Act 2009 provides that any person possessing such minimum qualification, as laid down by an Academic Authority, authorized by the Central Government, by notification, shall be eligible for appointment as a teacher. The Central Government vide notification dated 21st March 2010 declared National Council for Teacher Education (NCTE) as the Academic Authority under sec. 23 of RTE Act 2009 read with rule 17 of RTE Rules2010.

b. The NCTE vide notification dated 23rd August 2010 (**Appendix-1**) read with notification dated 29th July 2011 (**Appendix-2**) prescribed the minimum qualification for a person to be eligible for appointment as a teacher in classes I to VIII in a school as amended from time to time. Further, NCTE (Determination of Minimum Qualifications for Recruitment of Teachers in Schools) regulation 2014 (**Appendix-3**) read with rule 53 of Affiliation Bye- Laws prescribes minimum qualification for teachers upto classXII.

c. The Academic Authority i.e. NCTE under RTE Act 2009 also prescribes passing of Teacher Eligibility Test (TET) as essential qualification to be eligible for appointment as teacher of classes I toVIII.

2. Appointment of the Teachers:

a. The school shall ensure that all appointments be in accordance to rule 25 of Affiliation Bye-Laws and/or procedure prescribed in respective State/U.T. Act.

b. The school shall ensure that the vacancy of a teacher shall not exceed 10% of the total sanctioned strength of the teachers as required under sec. 28 of RTE Act2009.

3. Duties of the Teachers:

a. The school shall ensure that teachers are given specific academic duties as provided under sec. 24 (1) of RTE Act 2009, read with rule 21 (2) of RTE Rules2010.

b. Sec. 27 of RTE Act 2009 emphasizes that teachers should be free from deployment to non-educational assignments and enable teachers to spend more time on school and classroom related activities.This statutory provision has been reiterated vide M/o Human Resources Development, Govt. of India letter no. F-1-3/2010-EE4 dated 13th September 2010.The CBSE vide circular no. CBSE/Aff.04/Circular/2016 dated 28th October 2016 advised that the teachers may not be deployed for non-academicactivities.

c. No teacher shall engage in private tuition or private teaching activities as per sec. 28 of RTE Act 2009 and rule 39 of AffiliationBye-Laws.

d. As per Rule 10.5 and 32 of Affiliation Bye-Laws of the Board, normally a teacher should be engaged as a whole time employee in the school except in special cases wherein the work load does not justify a whole time teacher due to its unique nature. No teacher, teaching secondary and/or senior secondary classes, shall be required to teach more than ¾thof the total periods in a week. However, in case of schools offering the vocational courses, the school can engage subject expert/teacher on contract/part-time and share the resources with reputed/recognized institutions having expertise in such vocational courses.

4. Salary and Conditions of Service of the Teacher:

a. The scale of pay and allowances of teachers in the school shall be at par with the similar qualification, work and experience as provided under sec.23 (3) of RTE Act 2009 read with rule 20 (3) of RTE Rules 2010 and in accordance with rule 3.3 (i) (v) of Affiliation Bye-Laws. The salary and other allowances to the teachers shall be transferred through ECS on the last working day of the month.

b. In accordance with the provisions of rule 20 (2) of RTE Rules 2010 read with Chapter VII of Affiliation Bye-Laws, the school shall define and publish the terms and conditions of service of the teachers to create a professional cadre of teachers to impart quality education and ensure the learning outcomes to thestudents.

c. The school shall ensure timely promotion after completion of residency period and benefit of Modified Assured Career Progression (MACP) to its teachers at par with teachers working in the similar grade in Central/State Government schools.

d. The school shall prescribe transparent and objective Annual performance Appraisal system on the lines similar to APAR in respect of teachers under Central/State Government, which shall be the basis for promotion and/or MACP.

e. The school shall enter into a 'contract of service' with the teacher in accordance to Appendix III of Affiliation Bye-Laws or in the form prescribed by the State/U.T. Government, as the case maybe.

f. The school shall give due recognition to the academic responsibilities of the teachers and involve them in the educational activities in a dignifiedmanner.

g. The school shall not retain the original degree/ diploma certificates of the teachers after their appointment. Copies of degree/diploma certificates duly certified by the Head of School shall be placed in the personal file of the teacher in lieu of the original documents.

5. Retirement:

Every teacher including the Head of the School

shall superannuate from the service on attaining the age of 60 years as per rule 30.1 of Affiliation Bye-Laws. However, National Teacher awardees may be considered for further extension of service upto two years after attaining the age of superannuation subject to meritorious service, impeccable character, sound health, good leadership, management qualities and outstanding results throughout with the prior approval of the CBSE as stipulated in the circular no. CBSE/ Aff./Circular/5/2016 dated 20th December 2016.

6. Redressal of Grievance:

The school shall establish the internal 'Grievance Redressal Mechanism' for the teachers as mandated under sec. 24 (3) of RTE Act 2009.

7. Professional Development of the Teachers:

a. The school shall provide training facility for the teachers on similar lines as mandated under sections 8 (i) and 9 (j) of RTE Act 2009 regarding Appropriate Government and Local Authority respectively. Under rule 3.3(i) (vi) of Affiliation Bye-Laws, the school shall organize at least one-week training programme for the teachers in association with the Centers of Excellence (CoEs) established by the CBSE or any Teacher's Training Institute recognized by the Central/State Government.

b. The school shall ensure that the school library has appropriate books/periodicals useful for teachers and designate a dedicated area for them in the library to enrich their subject knowledge.

8. Sexual Harassment Committee:

The school shall constitute an 'Internal Complaints Committee' and take appropriate action as per the provisions of The Sexual Harassment of Women at Workplace (Prevention, Prohibition and Redressal) Act 2013.

9. Other Facilities for the Teachers:

The School shall ensure adequate provision for staff rooms, crèche facility, canteen facility and separate rest-rooms for the teachers.

Deputy Secretary (Affiliation)

COUNCIL FOR THE INDIAN SCHOOL CERTIFICATE EXAMINATIONS

Appointment, Service Conditions and Duties of the Teachers

1. Teaching Staff

(a) The teaching staff must be qualified and trained. The Council has laid down the minimum qualifications for the teaching staff (in Chapter II). In the case of certain subjects, the Council will take into consideration such qualifications as are necessary.

(b) The Governing Body / Managing Committee of the school shall issue a written appointment letter to every employee of the school. Unless otherwise stipulated by the State Government, the terms of service in the appointment letter shall incorporate the following aspects:

(i) the terms and conditions of service of the employee including the designation, scale of pay and other allowances, to which he/ she shall be entitled;

(ii) the schools in India must appoint, and pay salaries and other admissible allowances to the staff at par with the corresponding categories of employees in the State Government schools or as per conditions prescribed by the Government of India or as per the conditions laid down by the State Government in the NOC;

(iii) the schools outside India should pay salaries not lower than that of the teachers in government schools in that country;

(iv) the different categories of leave ofabsence, age of retirement, provident fund, pension, gratuity, medical and other benefits to which the employee shall be entitled;

(v) the penalties which could be imposed on the employee for the violation of any Code of Conduct or the Service Rules or the breach of any of the terms of the contract entered into by him/her;

(vi) the manner in which an employee can be suspended and disciplinary proceedings, in relation to an employee, shall be pursued before he/she can be dismissed, removed from service or reduced in rank;

(vii) arbitration of any dispute arising out of any breach of service conditions between the employee and the Governing Body / Managing Committee, with regard to terms and conditions of appointment, scales of pay and other allowances, leave of absence, age of retirement, pension, gratuity, provident fund, medical and other benefits, any disciplinary action leading to the suspension, dismissal or removal from service or reduction in rank of the employee or any other matter must be specified in suchcontract.

(c) A specimen copy of the Service Agreement, Code of Conduct and Service Rules referred to in (b) above with any subsequent amendments shall be forwarded to the Chief Executive and Secretary of the Council by the Governing Body/ Managing Committee of the School.

Bibliography

Primary sources

The holy Vedas

Upanishads

Village Education in India, 1920 published from Calcutta University

Nehru Jawaharlal, *Discovery of India,* Oxford University Press, New Delhi, 2002

Plato, *Republic,* Prakash Book, New Delhi, 2021 reprinted

Strong, W.F, *Dinajpur Gazetteer,* The Pioneer Press, 1912, Allahabad, First Reprinted by N.L. Publishers, Siliguri, Year of Reprint not mentioned

Lambern. E. G, *Malda Gazetteer,* Bengal Secretariat depot, Calcutta, 1819, First Reprinted by N.L Publishers, Siliguri, Year of Reprint not mentioned

Hunter. W.W. *A statistical Account of Darjeeling,* Reprinted by N.L. Publishers, Siliguri, 2012

Malley, O'S.S.L, *Purnia Gazetteer,* N.L. Publishers, Siliguri, 2011

Grunning, F. John, *Jalpaiguri Gazetteer,* N.L. Publishers, Siliguri, First Reprinted, 2008

Hunter, H.W, *A Statistical Account of Cooch Behar,* N.L publishers, Siliguri Reprinted 2012

Macaulay minute as accessed from www.archieve.org/details/Minutes201311

Sunder. E.H.D, Final Report on the survey and settlement of the western Duars in the District of Jalpaiguri, 1889-95 Edited by D.C. Roy, N. L. Publishers, Reprinted 2013

Malley, O.S.S.L, *Bengal district Gazetteer,* Logos press, Delhi, reprinted 1999.

A Final Report on the survey and settlement of Kalimpong government estate in the district of Darjeeling, 1901-1903, Calcutta, 1905

Secondary sources

English books :

Basham A L, *Wonder that was India,* Picador, London, 2004

Einstein Albert, *The world as I see,* Maple Press, Noida, 2021

Seith Leila, *On Balance,* Penguin, Gurgugram, 2010

Chakraborty Ranjan, *A History of Modern India,* Surjeet publication, New Delhi, 2019

Bhushan, Prashant, *The case that shook India,* Penguin, Gurugram, 2017

Laha, Binay, *Indology,* Vol I to Vol viii, local print

Mukhopadhya, Narayan, A study of the growth of western education in Bengal between 1919 and

1947 with particular reference to its influence upon the progress of Muslim and Women, Phd Thesis submitted in April 1981 at Calcutta University under the Supervision of Dr Suprakash Sanyal.

Gangopadhaya, Ashok, Uttar Bango parichay, Second edition, *Granthotirtho,* Kolkata, Second edition, 2003

Ghosh Arun, *Adhunik Bharatiya Sikkhar Itihas,* Educational Enterprise, Kolkata, reprinted 2011-12

On the Education of the people of India, London, Read books, 2006 (Reprint)

Forbes Geraldine, *Women in Modern India,* Cambridge University Press, Delhi, Reprint, 2018

Panikkar, N.K., *Culture, Ideology, Hegemony, Intellectual and social consciousness in Colonial India,* Anthem Press, London, second print 2001

Vidyasagar : The life and after life of an eminent Indian, Routledge (Manohar) 2014

Hatcher, A. Brian, *Hindu Widow Marriage,* Orient Black Swan Private Limited, New Delhi, 2012

Caste, Politics and the Raj : Bengal, 1872-1937, KP Bagchi & Company, 1990

Waterhouse, M. David, *The origins of Himalayan Studies, Briyan Houghton Hodgson in Nepal and Darjeeling (1820-1858),* Routledge Curzon, Taylor and Francis group, London and New work, 2005

Devee Sunity, *The autobiography of an Indian Princess, Maharani of Cooch Behar,* London, John Murrah, Albanarle Street, W. 1921

Basu, Swaraj, *Dynamics of a Caste Movement: The Rajbanshis of North Bengal (1910-1947),* Manohar Publishers and Distributors, New Delhi 2003

Diversified cropping pattern and Agricultural Development : A Case Study From Malda District, India, Springer Publications, 2021

Laha, Binay, *Act local think global,* Authors Press, New Delhi, 2019

Laha Binay, *The Wife of Red Soil,* Authors press, New Delhi, 2018

Laha Binay, Acharjee Krishnasankar, Ghosh Ratan, *Contemporary world English Poet,* Clever Fox, Chennai, 2021

Forbes Geraldine, *Women in Modern India,* Cambridge University Press, 2018

E. Sreedhran, *A Textbook of Historiography,* Orient Blackswan, Hyderabad, 2004

Sheering. M. A, *The history of Protestant Movement in India, 1706-1881,* Religious Tract Society, London, 1884.

Richter Julius, *A History of Missions in India,* London: Oliphant Anderson

Warnle Paul, *The beginning of Christianity,* Vol 1, Forgotten books, 2012

Sreedharan. E, *A text book of historiography,* Orient Blackswan, Hyderabad, 2004

Kumar Ranjit, *Research Methodology,* Sage Publication, New Delhi, 2014

Jean Dreze, Amartya Sen, *India: Economic Development and Social Opportunity,* Oxford University Press, Delhi, Seventh Edition, 1999

Journal of the Asiatic Society, Edited and published by Dr Satyabrata Chakraborty, April 2018, Kolkata.Vol Lx, No 1

Sarkar Mahua, *Environment and History, Recent Dialogues,* Kalpaz Publications, 2008, Delhi

Das Meenakshi and Bhuimali Anil, *Darjeeling Hill Economy,* Abhijeet Publications, Delhi

Das Aniruddha, Bengal Renaissance : Krishnanath College and the intelligentsia of Murshidabad, (1853-1953) the PhD thesis submitted by Aniruddha Das at Jadavpur University, 2008,available on shodhganga, http:hdt.handle.net/10603/166000

Dozey, E. C., *A concise history of Darjeeling district since 1835,* N. L. Publishers, Siliguri, Reprinted, 2011

Bond Ruskin, *Lone fox dancing,* Speaking Tiger, New Delhi, 2017

Sen Amartya, *The Argumentative Indian,* Penguin, New Delhi, 2006

Katju Markandey, *The shape of things to come,* Harper Collins, Noida, 2019

Sharma RS, *India's Ancient past,* Oxford India paperback, New Delhi, 2017

Azad K A Maulana, *India Wins Freedom,* Orient Black Swan, Delhi, 2015

Sisodia, Manish, *Shiksha,* Penguin Books, Gurugram, 2019

Tharoor, Sashi, *An Era of Darkness,* Aleph Book Company, New Delhi, 2016

Rickoff, Andrew J, Past and present of our common school education, Reply to president B. A. Hinsdale, With a brief sketch of the History of Elementary Education in India, leader printing company, America, publication date not mentioned

Habib Irfan, *Medieval India,* National Book Trust, New Delhi, 2007

Graham, Benjamin, *Intelligent Investor,* Harper, New York, 2019

Chand, Jagdish, *Education in Ancient and Medieval India,* Anshah Publication House, New Delhi, 2007

Shashtri Nilakanta, *History of South India,* New Delhi, 2009

Bengali Books :

Gangopadhaya Ashok, *Uttar Bango parichay,* Second edition, Granthotirtho, Kolkata, Second edition, 2003

Ghosh Arun, *Adhunik Bharatiya Sikkhar Itihas,* Educational Enterprise, Kolkata, reprinted 2011-12.

Sharma Umesh, Jalpaiguri Pourosabha: Ekso pochis bochhorer itibritto, Umesh Sharma, prokasak -Shree Mohan Ghosh, Mitra and Ghosh Publishers, Kolkata, 2009

Sen, Johor, *Himalaya charcha o Darjeeling Prosongo,* Chikitusi Prakashani, Kolkata, 2013

Chowdhury, Ray, Subir *Henri Derojio, Tar jibon o somoy,* National Book Trust, Kolkata, Reprint 2016

Mukhoyapadhya, Sadhan, Sakti, *Renesaser Aloi Bango Darshan,* Punascha, Kolkata, First edition, 2019

Ghosh Brindaban, *Uttar Dinajpurer Purakirti,* published by Registrar, The University of North Bengal, 2020

Roy Ranjan Nihar, *Bangalir Itihas,* Adi Porbo, 1425, Dey's publishing, Kolkata

Shastri Sibnath, *Ramtanu Lahiri o tatkalin bango somaj,* Edited by Jyotirmoy Ghosh, Punascha, Kolkata,2020

Ghosh Samit, *Dakshin Dinajpurer Purakirti, Sanskritik Oi tijyo o Itihas,* Amar Bharati, 2014

Gangopadhya Gautam, *Prachin Bharater Bhougolik Itibritto,* Ananda Prokashan, Reprint 2016

Roy Amalkanti, *Gaur Ramkeli,* Deep Prakashani, Kolkata, 2017

Interview :

Interview with Rajib Ghosh Roy, pgt at DPS taken on 16/09/2021

Interview with Indranil Banerjee, principle of Imperial Academy, Indore, Madhya Pradesh taken on several times in the month of August to September 2021

Interview with Vijay Mahantesh A Hosur taken several times in the month of August and September 2021

Interview with Pankaj Bhalla, a senior most teacher in Karnal, Haryana, taken several times in the month of August and September 2021

Interview with Jagdiswar Biradar, a former teacher from Karnataka taken on 6th September, 2021

Interview with Samidh Biswas, a pgt from west Bengal taken several times in the month of July, August 2021

Interview with Niraj Makwana, a pgt from Rajasthan, taken few times in the month of September 2021

Interview with Dr Sunita Singh taken on 7 th September 2021

Interview of various school managements, principals Teachers, Alumnai and different individuals taken for neccesary purposes.

Webliography :

www.cbse.nic.in

www.icse.ac.in

http://shodhganga.inflibnet.ac.in/handle/10603/159803

htt://saras. case. gov. in/cbse-aff/schdir-Report/userview.aspx

www.archieve.org

www.jstor.org

www.shodhganga.inflibnet.in

■■■■